L.I.F.E. Guide for

A Workbook for Living in Freedom Everyday

in Sexual Wholeness and Integrity

Heath B. Wise, M.A.

with core material by
Mark Laaser

Mark Laaser, Ph.D., Editor
L.I.F.E. Guides for Living in Freedom Everyday

L.I.F.E. Guide for Young Women
by Heath B. Wise, M.A.

Printed in the United States of America

ISBN 978-0-9816796-09

NOTE: This workbook is not intended to provide therapy, counseling, clinical advice or treatment, or to take the place of clinical advice and treatment from a professional mental health provider or personal physician. Readers are advised to consult qualified healthcare providers regarding mental, emotional and medical issues. Neither the publisher, the author, nor L.I.F.E. Ministries assumes any responsibility for any possible consequences from any reader's action or application of information in this workbook.

Color House Graphics
www.colorhousegraphics.com

What you are holding in your hand is made possible because of collaboration between XXXchurch.com and L.I.F.E Ministries International.

About XXXchurch.com

XXXchurch exists to bring light in the midst of the dark, shallow and superficiality within a culture that has been affected by pornography. The thrust is to bring awareness, openness, accountability and recovery to the church, society and individuals who have been affected by pornography. Through non-judgmental and creative means X3church delivers this message of hope and healing.

The Team
Craig Gross is the founder and leader of XXXchurch.com. Working alongside Craig is an amazing group of people including J.R. Mahon, Clint McManamam, Brandon Piety, Rob Supan, Ginny Spears, , Michelle Truax, Laci Warne and some great interns and volunteers.

The Name
XXXchurch is provocative, memorable, and it combines the seedy and the sacred. Enough said.

The Mission
XXXchurch is here to make you think, react and to decide where you stand on the issues of porn. We're not here to sling mud, but to shove the envelope and try and do some good.

The Tag Line
The "#1 Christian Porn Site" is what we are.

The Vibe
It's hip, relevant, irreverent, honest, fun and designed for people just like you.

International Headquarters:
XXXchurch.com
PO Box 150169
Grand Rapids, MI 49515
United States
Phone/Fax 616-588-5988
info@xxxchurch.com

About L.I.F.E. Ministries International (Living In Freedom Everyday)

A Support Group Ministry for those recovering from inappropriate sexual behavior.

The mission of L.I.F.E. Ministries International is to Encourage, Empower and Equip God's people to live everyday in sexual integrity. L.I.F.E. works with church leadership to offer a safe place to recover from sexual addiction and brokenness.

The L.I.F.E. Guide series of workbooks all feature Dr. Laaser's seven Biblical principles, tailored from classic 12 step recovery group experience. Accountability within transparent relationships in a "safe" environment is the strength of the support group method in dealing with this "secret sin" of the church. Dr. Laaser calls these workbooks the "most complete workbook" available to the Christian community.

L.I.F.E. Ministries International is dedicated to bringing to the church and to Christian Counselors the understanding that Biblically based support group programs, such as L.I.F.E. groups, are essential to bring the full healing and restorative power of Jesus to those struggling to recover from inappropriate sexual behavior.

You can find out more about L.I.F.E. Ministries at **www.freedomeverday.org**

Congratulations on purchasing this workbook from XXXchurch! XXXchurch and L.I.F.E. Ministries have collaborated to offer the L.I.F.E. Guide series in response to the growing problem of inappropriate sexual behavior in our culture and in the church today. In addition to the series of support group workbooks, L.I.F.E. offers leadership materials and other resources to help you get the most from your journey to sexual integrity.

We encourage you to visit our website at **www.freedomeveryday.org** to:

- Learn more about starting a L.I.F.E. Support Group
- Get resources for use in your Support Group
- Interact with other Group Members and Group Facilitators

Please register with L.I.F.E. Ministries, on our website or using the convenient form below, so we can enter you in our data base and provide you with the information and on-going supportive relationship that helps ensure your recovery. We also encourage you to list your group on our website so others can learn who and where you are.

For more information, you can also call our toll free pre-recorded Information Helpline at (866) 408-LIFE.

Name: ______________________________

Address: ______________________________

City/State/Zip: ______________________________

Email: ______________________________

L.I.F.E. Group meets (if applicable): Day: __________ Time: ______________

Location: ______________________________

Address: ______________________________

City/State/ZIP: ______________________________

Contact name and phone: ______________________________

L.I.F.E. MINISTRIES INTERNATIONAL
P.O. Box 952317
Lake Mary, FL 32795
VOICE: (866) 408-5433; FAX: (407) 840-9730
www.freedomeveryday.org

To Encourage, Empower, and Equip God's people to Live In Freedom Everyday.

Foreword from L.I.F.E Ministries

Sexual dysfunction has become a common cancer within today's culture, and the church is certainly not exempt. The number of people struggling with sexual brokenness has sky-rocketed due to two main factors: the prevalence and availability of pornography and a sexually saturated media. Mark Laaser has commented that our entire society is being ***sexually abused*** by this onslaught. Unhealthy and un-scriptural sexual behaviors such as pornography, compulsive masturbation and promiscuity are just as prevalent among Christian young people as they are in the society at large. Among believers, there are young men and young women—including future leaders—who, because of painful experiences and sinful choices, compulsively use sex and unholy relationships as a key to popularity and acceptance or as an escape or medication to help them cope with life. The consequences of these behaviors can be devastating to the strugglers and also to their families and friends.

Many of those who struggle with life dominating sexual behaviors desperately long to be free from their bondage and intensely desire to live in sexual integrity. They want to be Living In Freedom Everyday. The *L.I.F.E. Guide* workbook series is written to help God's people be free from the bondage of sexual addiction and to equip them to walk in His unconditional love and defining truth. L.I.F.E. Ministries is grateful to have Dr. Mark Laaser, an internationally known author and leader in the area of sexual addiction recovery, as the author of the *L.I.F.E. Guide for Men* and the general editor of the *L.I.F.E. Guide* series. Dr. Laaser conceptualized the Seven Principles on which each workbook is based. A respected expert in a specific area of ministry—women, adolescents, spouses—then adapts the material for that target population. This design provides consistency of information and terminology throughout the *L.I.F.E. Guide* series.

This *L.I.F.E. Guide for Young Women* is the fifth in the *L.I.F.E. Guide* series. It is dedicated to helping our young women win the battle against the rampant sexuality that permeates our culture and our commerce in these times. In so many ways this onslaught is targeted directly at our young people, through entertainment, advertising and fashion. It is our hope that this guide will equip the young women of our churches and our communities to prevail against that attack and to become the sexually pure leaders of tomorrow.

The L.I.F.E. Ministries support group program offers Christ-centered and relationally oriented groups that incorporate spiritual discipline, small group accountability and ongoing prayer and support to those struggling with sexual brokenness. L.I.F.E. Groups are support groups not therapy groups. While there is much within each of the L.I.F.E. Guides and the recommended recovery materials to help the struggler identify and deal with the wounds from the past, we also encourage individual therapy to address root issues and heal the woundedness that often leads to sexual addiction. The critical ongoing support comes from the networking together of lives in real relationships—open, transparent, and accountable connections with fellow strugglers. L.I.F.E. Groups value confidentiality, with an absolute commitment to a safe atmosphere for complete honesty; and complete acceptance, where members are embraced in an attitude of love and forgiveness by others sharing common struggles. All of this is "Guiding" the group members toward Christ-centered sexuality, under the conviction that our true sexual identity is found in the freedom and grace that only Jesus can offer.

Registration With L.I.F.E. Ministries

We encourage all groups using this *L.I.F.E. Guide* workbook to become registered L.I.F.E. Groups. Registering your L.I.F.E. Group with L.I.F.E. Ministries International will entitle your group leadership to access additional information and discounted resources, and opens additional communication links for information about conferences, workshops, leadership training and other benefits--often at substantial discounts. Through newsletters and the L.I.F.E. Ministries website, your group leaders will have access to materials and information to help your L.I.F.E. Group grow and to expand your sexual addiction ministry within your church and your community. Your group will also be listed in our network of L.I.F.E. Groups and other sexual addiction ministries, so those looking for help in your community can find it, and your group members will never be without needed support when away from home. Finally, by registering, your group will be furthering the work of L.I.F.E. Ministries International, and will help make this support group ministry available in additional churches and communities across the country and around the world.

To find more information, to start a L.I.F.E. Group, or to register your L.I.F.E. Group; checkout the website, call L.I.F.E. Ministries toll-free, or write for more information. We would love to welcome you and start you on the journey toward Living In Freedom Everyday in His unconditional love.

L.I.F.E. Ministries International
P.O. Box 952317
Lake Mary, FL 32795
866-408-LIFE (866-408-5433)
www.freedomeveryday.org

Foreword by Mark Laaser, Ph.D.

Like all of the L.I.F.E. guides, the Young Women's Guide is greatly needed. It is the right timing. Young women today are being virtually assaulted all the time with unhealthy and sinful messages. One has only to read the titles of articles on the most popular of teenage magazines to see what those messages are. Girls are being told that they need to dress in certain provocative ways. The word modesty is probably not in their vocabulary. They are also being told that they need to be sexually aggressive and find ways to get boys to sexually pursue them. It's really true to say that all of the old messages that boys used to tell each other have been passed on to the girls.

Some of us familiar with brain chemistry believe that young women's brains are literally being re-wired. We used to think that women weren't attracted to pornography. We used to think that girls didn't masturbate. We now know that both of these beliefs just aren't true. It's as if young women's brain are adjusting away from the way God created it to be. As a result girls are becoming increasingly sexually active at earlier ages. The average age that a girl starts menstruation has even dropped as if her body is trying to keep up with this fact. Christian girls are not exempt. Various studies have indicated that they're just as active and perhaps more creative in the ways that they are.

It is one of the greatest challenges of our time to find ways to help our young women combat the assault of culture all around them. More of us need to be writing about this even if we don't think we have all the answers. We must take the risk to inspire girls to be sexually pure until marriage. We can't just tell them to "not do it." We have to tell them why. We must give them a vision of the importance of waiting. For every "no" we tell them, there must be a "yes." We need practical tools.

So, it is with pleasure that I encourage you to use this guide with groups of young women. It is always in fellowship that we find healing and wholeness. Heath Wise has done a wonderful job in taking on this important challenge. The exercises in this book with help young women truly know themselves, understand their own need for God, and seek concrete ways to lead the life that God calls them to. These are not the patent simplistic answers that we were told. This is a book that will inspire honesty and true dependence on God and others.

Congratulations Heath on accepting one of the great challenges of our day. I pray that thousands will benefit from it.

L.I.F.E Guide for Young Women
Table of Contents

Author's Acknowledgements and Dedication

There are many reasons why I decided to participate in this project and write this young woman's guide. But chief among them was the fact that I have three children who are the light of my life. They have brought such immeasurable joy to my life over the years and have taught me much about living life in this postmodern world. As I think about the challenges that my daughter and sons face as they live in this sexualized culture, I want to do what I can to empower their journey.

Of course, this series would not even be possible without the work of Dr. Mark Laaser. He has so effectively pioneered this work with his teaching, writing, speaking and counseling practice. I can never thank him enough for the impact that he has had in my own life personally as well as the lives of so many of my clients. His integrity, faithfulness and perseverance in getting sober and staying the course of recovery gives hope to countless people who are struggling with sexual integrity issues. His life is a powerful testimony to the power of God to change lives.

Richard Blankenship has taught me most of what I know about this field. He is a gifted therapist. I am constantly amazed as I see his instincts and wisdom with his clients. He has been my mentor over these years but more importantly, my friend. He has encouraged and believed in me even though I was unsure of myself. What a gift that has been to me as he has supported and cheered for me. I so appreciate the way that he has valued me enough to let me do therapy the way that I think is best. His confidence inspires me to excellence.

How do you say thank you to the people that made this whole project possible? Bob and Johna Hale and their wonderful staff at L.I.F.E. ministries have provided the vision, energy and backing for this project. Without them, none of this would be possible. It is their passionate desire to see people living in freedom everyday. And it is their commitment to this project that is making that possible for many men and women. For me personally, I am so grateful for their kind patience extended to me during a difficult time in my life. Thank you from the bottom of my heart for your grace and care.

Many thanks go to the staff at North Atlanta Center for Christian Counseling, particularly Joyce Tomblin and Mark Richardson. They faithfully do their work because they love the clients that they work with. They truly want to see them whole and free. They challenge me to be a better therapist.

Marcia McDaniel tirelessly edited and perfected this manuscript. Her expertise and suggestions enabled me to focus on other aspects of the writing. She stepped in at a time that I needed help the most. Thank you, Marcia.

And lastly, I want to thank Debby Harrison. She has challenged me over the years to think about these issues. She has a heart for women and a heart for freedom. She sharpens me as she asks me questions and probes for answers, constantly pushing me to God and making me want to know Him more. She has been such a faithful friend, praying for me and fighting on my behalf, loving me and always seeing the best in me. She has taught me more about being a counselor than any other person I know. I will be forever grateful for the gift of her friendship.

This book is dedicated to the scores of young women who have been caught in the cycle of addiction and sexual sin and have courageously fought to get free. Their lives both challenge and inspire me.

Letter to Parents

As a parent myself, I have much compassion for parents today. It is such a threatening world that we live in and most parents fear for the safety of their child. And most fear that their child will make choices that will harm them or scar them for the rest of their lives. I talk to so many parents who are confused about how to help their child. They want to be good parents but they do not know what to do. You might be the parent who is desperately hurting because you have done all you know to do and nothing seems to help. Or you might be the parent who never suspected that anything was wrong. The fact that you are reading this letter, tells me that you are a good parent. You care about what your daughter is reading and doing. My prayer is that you will be able to be supportive during this journey.

You might have some questions when you see the topic of the workbook. It is addressing sexual integrity issues. I have found that nothing causes more anxiety for a parent than finding out that their daughter is struggling with sexual integrity. But the good news is that there is hope. This workbook will help her get to the root of the issue and begin to make changes. It will help her to stay sexually pure and to have a vision of the kind of woman she wants to be. She will look at her identity and who God says that she is. She will learn to have supportive, healthy relationships that encourage her to be healthy and whole.

The best way for you to be supportive is to come alongside and be willing to talk if your daughter wants to talk. Do not force her to tell you everything if she does not want to do so. Be a safe person for her so that she will talk to you when she is ready. Pray for her. Sometimes in their fear, parents can come on strong and shame their children. Remember, the Bible says that it is the kindness of God that leads to repentance.

As threatening as it is, be thankful that she is talking to someone and working on the issue. I always think it is a good idea for parents to be informed. Buy a copy of the workbook yourself so that you can see what she is doing. But don't intrude on her privacy by reading hers. Take this opportunity to educate yourself about addictions so that you can understand your child. Get general updates from the leader as the group progresses. Remember, our children are always being influenced for good and for evil. There is so much negative influence, aren't you thankful to have other people who are willing to influence her for good? This is a battle and we need to work together; it is tiring to try to do it alone.

Sometimes parents are concerned because there are secrets in the family that everyone is trying to hide. Addiction is a family disease because it affects the whole family. If one suffers, the whole family suffers. You know this yourself because you have undoubtedly been affected by your daughter's struggle. Addictions often run in families. So there might be other family members who are also struggling. There is no shame if that is the case. There is help available. There are women's and men's L.I.F.E. groups available as well as other resources for other addictions. Please get help if you need it and join your daughter on her journey of recovery.

INTRODUCTION

By Heath Wise, M.A.

Allie is a typical teenager, active in church and school activities. She appears to have plenty of friends and a close family. When there is something that needs to be done at church, Allie is quick to volunteer and always does a good job at whatever she is asked to do. People would describe her as sweet, confident and happy. But Allie has a painful secret. She is sleeping with her boyfriend and cannot seem to stop. In fact, this is not the first guy that she has slept with. "I keep thinking that if I just pray enough or read my Bible more, I will be able to stop," Allie says. "But it never seems to work. I cry and cry and beg the Lord to help me but I just do it again. Why can't I stop?"

Maybe you can identify with Allie. The details might be different but the struggle is the same. You really want to be sexually pure and have made promises to yourself and God but have not been able to keep them. Sometimes it seems like you are on a rollercoaster, doing well for awhile and then falling again. You wonder why other people don't seem to struggle the way you do. You feel ashamed and wonder if the Christian life just doesn't work for you because you are so messed up inside.

Well, I have good news. There is hope for you! This book is about learning to live in freedom everyday. And that is possible! This is not another self help or abstinence program. Those have their places. This is a different approach, one that many people have found very effective. You will learn about addiction and how to break that rollercoaster cycle. There are reasons that you have been struggling with your sexuality. You are not just a bad person who will never get it together.

There is so much confusion about what it means to be a woman in today's society. Our culture tells us that to be a woman you have to be desirable sexually to a man. Look at the commercials on television. Sex sells everything from soap to cars. A provocative woman is seen as the ideal. It doesn't matter if the woman has character or intelligence. Her whole value is wrapped up in being sexual. Her whole identity is a sexual identity tied to her body image. Instead of having an internal sense of her identity and worth, a woman in this system is dependent on external validation. Do men find her attractive? Then she must be. Do men look at her body? Then she must have value. She has to have the approval of men who find her desirable. This is such a trap. External validation of identity never works. It will never be enough; she has to keep looking to see if another man finds her attractive and then another.

In response to our highly sexualized culture, the church often takes a negative view of sexuality. The motive is a good one. They want to save young people from making mistakes that wound them and cause scars. But even though the motive is a good one, the result is not helpful. We come down hard on sex and teach young people to shut down their sexual feelings until they can get married. Seems like a good idea but it doesn't work. Or we just don't talk about it at all which sends a message that sex is shameful. And one of the most damaging things that we do is to join the culture in making women sex objects.

When my own daughter was a teenager, I remember so many talks at retreats and church events about girls being careful about the way that they dress because it made it difficult for the guys. The underlying assumption is that guys are sexual beings and that they are going to lust. But it shifts the responsibility for the guys' lust onto the girls. They are sex objects that need to be covered up so that they don't cause the guys to sin. Don't misunderstand me. I think girls need to be careful about the way they dress. But when I see a skimpily clad young woman, I am saddened not because she is making it difficult for some guy, but because it tells me what she believes about herself and where she gets her value. We are totally missing the heart of the issue for men and the women.

God made you a woman and He intends for you to delight in the creation that He has made. Being female is a large part of who you are. Learning how to celebrate your sexuality as a female and still remain pure is part of what you will be learning in this book. You don't have to act out sexually to know how valuable you are. God made you female and that is a glorious thing!

HOW TO USE THIS L.I.F.E. *Guide*

This book is designed as a guide for your journey of healing from the shame and grief of broken sexuality. Whether you found it on your own, on the Web, or from a LIFE group, our prayer is that you'll be able to enjoy the strength of fellowship with other young men who desire to live in freedom everyday. Take yourself to a quiet place, listen to God's leading in your life, and make a firm commitment that you'll and follow his leading in your journey.

This is your private book. It's for your use in your journey towards sexual purity. You might need a journal in which to do assignments. Put your name on the journal and keep it in a safe place. Because of the level of honesty you might need to keep this book and your journal locked in a safe place. Uninvited readers may not be safe and can misinterpret your words and do much damage. This work is for you. You might at some point want to share your experience in these exercises with a parent, youth pastor, accountability group, or in other relationships where you feel safe. However, don't let anyone pressure you into sharing your journal.

The LIFE Guide can be used in a group where support and accountability are in place. It can be used with a friend or in a class setting. When using it in a group it might be good to have a safe adult you can consult with in the event assistance is needed. Teachers can use this book in classroom settings while studying the subject of sexuality. One format in a large class might be to divide people into smaller groups and let them share the work they do on the exercises in a safe setting. Another might be to work the book one-on-one with an accountability partner. Youth pastors might want to use this material in working individually with young men. Before each session read the introductory material on the L.I.F.E. principle and complete the exercise. Come prepared to share your answers with your group or partner. Also come prepared to share any struggles and victories you might have experienced since your last meeting.

The assignments will take you deeper into the work of each LIFE principle. You'll need your journal and your workbook as you do the exercises. There are three exercises for each L.I.F.E. principle. Do them in order. This is a journey in which each principle builds on the other.

L.I.F.E. Guide Safety Guidelines

This book will talk about safe relationships with accountability partners. Don't rush out and set up a sexual accountability group. These are guidelines for L.I.F.E. accountability groups. It's absolutely essential that every L.I.F.E. Group be a safe place in which members can be honest and build healthy relationships. All group members are responsible for observing these Safety Guidelines. If they are violated, the group members must confront one another in love. If an individual cannot observe the guidelines consistently or after being confronted, he will be asked to leave the meeting. The well-being of the entire group is more important than any individual member. The L.I.F.E. guidelines are as follows:

1. It's safe to be honest. We expect all group members to tell the truth.

2. It's safe to have feelings. All feelings are acceptable to God and to the group.

3. We will allow safe group conversation with no graphic sexual descriptions or identifying specific clubs, web sites, movies, or pornographic books and magazines. We give each other feedback as long as it reflects our own experience, strength, and hope. Therefore, we begin our feedback with "I" and not with "you."

4. We don't preach. It's acceptable to share messages of spiritual strength and hope, to quote scripture, and to make statements about God. We avoid comments that use words like "should," "always," or "never," and expressions such as "God says . . .", "God's will for your life is . . .," or "God will be angry if . . ." We all seek to follow Christ in our own way.

5. We don't shame ourselves and others. We don't put down ourselves or others.

6. We don't blame anyone for our sinful behavior or our addiction. We focus on accepting responsibility for our actions and working on personal growth.

7. We abide by the principle of group confidentiality. We don't reveal the identity of other group members or any personal information outside the group. The only exception is if someone discloses that he intends to harm himself or someone else, including minor children or the elderly or disabled, we will take all necessary action outside of the LIFE group to report that danger and secure the safety of others. This might involve notifying a youth group leader, pastor, counselor, or proper authorities. These are the only exceptions to maintaining group confidentiality.

8. Try to secure a safe adult mentor to be available if necessary. This could be a parent, youth pastor, pastor, teacher, or counselor. Sometimes the level of emotional honesty can be difficult to cope with. There is no shame in asking for help. It would be good at the start of the group if members could identify who this individual will be.

The Mission of L.I.F.E.

Ours is a fellowship of young women who sincerely desire to abstain from sinful sexual and relational behavior and to present lives holy and pure before God. Many of us have been trapped in the vicious cycle of addictive sexuality. The lifestyle of sexual and relational fantasy, ritual, sexual sin, and grief has left us feeling out of control. We identify with the words of Paul in Romans 7:19.

"I know that nothing good lives in me, that is, in my sinful nature. For I have the desire to do what is good, but I cannot carry it out. For what I do is not the good that I want to do; no, the evil I do not want to do - - this I keep on doing. What a wretched man I am!"
Romans 7:19

We realize that our sin has grown worse over time. We have been addicted to the high of our lust, our sexual activity, fantasies, and relationships. We have not been able to stop despite the consequences, and we experience great shame.

Sexual acting out involves a history of secrecy, deceit, broken commitments, and potential harm to ourselves and others. All through life, we truly sought love and nurturing. We've been angry because we felt unloved. We have even been angry with God for not removing temptations, pain, and problems. We have substituted sex or an unholy relationship for love, thinking that the high of these affording pleasures would erase our true needs of communion with God, a relationship with Christ, and genuine connection with healthy others.

Many of us have promised, "This is the last time I'll act out," only to find that temptation and addiction would soon overtake us again. Don't be discouraged. You're not alone. Those of us who have chosen to become honest about our past and our emotions are experiencing healing with the help of the Holy Spirit. Many of us have tried to recover through our own thinking and on our own. We've even tried to manipulate God's healing through constant prayer, Bible studies, and church attendance. We are finding that God will help us heal only if we are truly willing to submit to His will by keeping ourselves humble and accountable.

If you desire what we have and are willing to go to any lengths to get it, we invite you to join us in the fellowship of L.I.F.E. - living in freedom everyday - with the help of our all loving and all powerful God, through His son Jesus Christ.

Seven Principles for L.I.F.E.

Following are the principles we follow as a path for overcoming sexual wounds, sin, and addiction.

1. We admit that we have absolutely no control of our lives. Sexual sin has become unmanageable.

2. We believe in God, accept the grace offered through his son Jesus Christ, and surrender our lives and our wills to Him on a daily basis.

3. We make a list of our sins and weaknesses and confess those to a person of spiritual authority.

4. We seek accountability and to build our character as children of God.

5. We explore the damage we have done, accept responsibility, and make amends for our wrongs.

6. In fellowship with others we develop honest, intimate relationships, where we celebrate our progress and continue to address our weaknesses.

7. As we live in sexual integrity, we carry the message of Christ's healing to those who still struggle, and we pursue a vision of God's purpose for our lives.

How Did This Happen To Me And Why Can't I Stop?

How do people from good Christian homes end up struggling with the same sexual issues as people in the world? We live in the same culture and are inundated with the same cultural stimulation. Why do some Christians seem to cope better than others? The answer may be found in understanding the addictive nature of sexuality, especially for people predisposed towards addiction due to genetic structure of the brain or from the family system where they live. If you have an addiction it's more than simply coping with sexual sin. The battle for an addict involves dealing with both sin and addiction. This concept, which has been critical in the healing journey of many, will be explained throughout this book.

Don't get caught up in trying to figure out whether or not you're an addict. The fact is, you're reading this book because you've struggled. The concepts will help you in your healing journey regardless of what you call the problem. The journey of living in freedom everyday isn't only possible, it's exciting, hopeful and rewarding. The treadmill of sexual acting out can be exchanged for sexual purity. The journey of overcoming compulsive behaviors and controlling your thoughts won't be easy, but it's the most rewarding journey you'll ever take. It will impact your life in ways that go far beyond sexuality.

No matter how much praying, fasting, and Bible study takes place, the unmanageability of sexual acting out can make it seem like transformation is impossible. It may be that you're experiencing shame over lack of control. People may say things like "can't you just choose to do the right thing?" Or, "Just do what the Bible tells you to do, and you'll be ok." Most sexual addicts know what the Bible says and have tried everything within their power to get their lives under control. Scriptures like "flee from sexual immorality" 1 Corinthians 6:18) and "there must not be even a hint of sexual immorality" (Ephesians 5:3) become sources of frustration instead of healing.

Paul may not have been a sex addict, but he clearly knew what it was like to struggle with the unmanageable. You can take comfort in realizing that one of the great spiritual leaders of the Bible struggled with the same feelings that frustrate you in your quest for sexual purity.

"I do not understand what I do. For what I want to do I do not do, but what I hate, I do. For I have the desire to do what is good, but I cannot carry it out. For what I do is not the good I want to do; no, the evil I do not want to do - this I keep on doing." "Now if I do what I do not want to do, it is no longer I who do it, but it is sin living in me that does it. What a wretched man I am."

Romans 7:15, 18-20, 24

When you struggle unsuccessfully with a problem, realize you're in some pretty good company. Understanding that addiction is a disease can provide some relief in understanding why the struggle is so difficult. There are factors at work that make it difficult to view this struggle as a simple matter of choice. We'll consider some of these factors in this section.

Disease Of Addiction

The disease concept of addiction has been around since the early 1800's, made popular by one of the signers of the Declaration of Independence, Dr. Benjamin Rush. It took until the 1970's and 80's for the disease model to be understood. Today our culture readily accepts this model in understanding drug and alcohol addiction. But what about sexual addiction?

Dr. John Sealy of UCLA defines addiction as "A pathological relationship with a mood-altering experience associated with denial of adverse consequences and loss of control." A "pathological" relationship is one that's unhealthy and destructive. From this we can understand the idea of disease. A "mood altering experience" can cover substance and behavioral addictions including addictions to Internet pornography. Different moods can trigger sexual acting out. Sexual stimulation and experience will alter one's mood. The rush of adrenaline can elevate the mood much like a runner experiences during a race. "With denial of adverse consequences" is also a trademark of addiction. Knowing that something is harmful will not stop an addict from engaging in that behavior. The knowledge that smoking can result in health problems has not stopped millions of addicts from self-harm. Addicts are so desperate for their "fix" that the consequences aren't considered when one craves mood alteration. "Loss of control" is a universal feature of any addiction. Sexual addiction is both obsessive and compulsive. In the moment of acting out, an addict believes that the compulsive behavior will put his mind to rest. This is why people will continue to harm themselves when it makes no sense. The result is despair and shame that fuels the cycle of addiction. Without identifying the cycle and attacking specific behaviors, the cycle will continue indefinitely.

Susan writes, "I don't want to be hooked on this stuff [Internet pornography]. But when I'm bored I start having fantasies. I can't get them out of my head. Even though I know better, I eventually give in and surf the Web until I get my fill of chat rooms. The guys sound so warm and inviting. In the end, I feel sick. Even though my brain tells me I'll feel sick afterwards, when the craving hits I have to fill it."

Neurochemistry

Another feature of addiction that we see in sexual acting out involves the concept of "tolerance." Most people are familiar with how this works with drugs and alcohol. The first time someone drinks alcohol he may immediately feel good. If alcohol is consumed on a daily basis it will take a higher volume than what was consumed the first time to get the same reaction. This is the concept of "tolerance." The more you consume, the more it will take to get high. Sexual acting out works the same way. The first time Susan went in to an Internet chat room she was immediately aroused and enjoyed the sensations that followed. Today Susan spends several hours on the Web to achieve the same "high" that she got the first time she entered a chat room. This is the result of developing tolerance. The brain gets used to being stimulated regularly through pictures, fantasies, and orgasms. If the addiction continues, it will take more of the "drug" to get high.

Neurochemistry involves the study of the brain and the role of the chemicals produced by the brain. Ingesting a substance would be an obvious way to alter the chemistry of the brain. Can looking at images or engaging in sexual behavior alter the brain? New studies of brain images reveal that fantasy and looking at images can produce addictive chemicals in the brain. Instead of taking chemicals from the outside, as with drugs or alcohol, the sex addict carries his own supply of the drug in his brain.

Without trying to sound like a medical textbook, I'll try to explain in simple terms the neurochemical reactions involved with sexual acting out. Sexual stimulation causes certain chemicals to increase in the brain. Many addicts struggle with boredom, depression, and attention deficit hyperactivity disorder. The influx of adrenaline makes levels of dopamine increase. Dopamine is the "James Brown" ("I feel good!") of neurotransmitters. Many addicts have stimulus seeking brains. They don't tolerate boredom. Their brains are working from the time they get up until they go to bed. The high risk nature of sexual acting out can create a surge in dopamine that elevates the mood of an addict. In desperation an addict will throw caution to the wind to feel better.

Skin to skin contact with other human beings releases oxytocin into the brain. Oxytocin creates feelings of pleasure and relaxation. Catecholamines are opiate like substances released in the brain during the feeling of ecstasy from sexual acting out. Dopamine, oxytocin, and catecholamines are produced as basic biological reactions to sexual stimulation of various kinds.

Brain studies also reveal that the brain of a sex addict will respond much like the brain of a crack cocaine addict. The sex addict simply carries around his own supply of chemicals. How convenient, huh? Unlike crack cocaine, these chemicals are legal. Unfortunately, they can be deadly in other ways.

When you struggle with sexually addictive behavior, it's more than a behavioral addiction. It creates a chemical dependency. To quote Dr. Mark Laaser, "Biological desire will never be satisfied biologically." In other words, there isn't enough sex in the world to satisfy the desire for more. This explains why sexual addiction is more than "just a choice." It involves a chemical reaction that creates an added battle for the sex addict to fight.

Understanding Sexual Behavior

Where do you draw the line between normal experimentation and addictive acting out? One one end of the spectrum, sexual behavior may stop at self-exploration. Others may get too involved too often and end up experiencing consequences. Some will become compulsive sex addicts. Regardless of where you are on the spectrum, if you want to stop acting out, the principles in this book will help you reach your goal of sexual health.

Lust and Temptation

Sexual thoughts and feelings are normal. They are not inherently sinful. Sexual feelings are a sign that you are growing and developing and your body is normal. God created your body to respond sexually. It is how he designed you. Psalm 139:13 says that God knit you together in the womb of your mother. A skilled "knitter" does very precise work by hand. He/she creates a unique individual masterpiece. As the master creator, God didn't make a mistake when he created your sexuality. Sexual response needs to be embraced as a healthy gift from your creator.

Temptation is not a sin. Matthew 4:1-11 shares the story of Jesus experiencing Temptation. Experiencing temptation doesn't mean you have crossed the line into sexual acting out. Thoughts and feelings do not automatically mean that you are committing adultery in your heart. Jesus was not sinning by experiencing temptation. Good news – neither are you!

> "No temptation has seized you (or Jesus) except what is common to man.
> And God is faithful; he will not let you be tempted beyond what you
> Can bear. But when you are tempted, he will also provide a way out so that
> You can stand up under it." (*1 Corinthians 10:13*)

Temptation is not an "if" it is a "when." Lust and temptation are a part of our lives today just as they were in the days of Jesus. And we must continue to seek God's way of escape and his strength to stand up under the pressures of a sexualized culture.

Masturbation

Masturbation is a word that can silence a conversation very quickly. The word itself is intimidating and can produce feelings of shame. Masturbation is the act of stimulating one's genitals for arousal and orgasm. A better term would be self-stimulation. The word masturbation was developed by the Catholic church several centuries ago. It was used as a value judgment to describe the act of self-stimulation. The word masturbation literally means "self-abuse". It was meant to control behavior that the church had labeled as sinful. This partly explains why the term is so shaming. The term is being used throughout this book because it is commonly understood in our culture.

The terms masturbation and self-stimulation are not found in the bible. The act of self-stimulation is never described in scriptures. Some have misused the story of Onan (Genesis 38:8-9) to say that masturbation is rebellion against God. The story of Onan does not involve self-stimulation. It is about a man having sexual intercourse and ejaculating on the ground instead of impregnating his brother's wife.

God has created many wonderful things in this world that have been misused and abused.
As a writer, counselor, and teacher, I cannot in good conscience begin to make rules where God has not. There are some times where masturbation becomes harmful. These must be distinguished from normal healthy self-exploration.

Self-exploration is a normal part of growing up. Your body was not designed to be a source of shame. The good feelings that come from self-stimulation can be exciting and frightening at the same time. It's normal to be curious about your body and how it functions.

There are times when masturbation can become problematic. As was said earlier, many positive things that God created have been misused. Self-stimulation is one of those activities that can be normal and healthy. It can also become destructive if it is misused and abused.

At what point does masturbation become a problem? Where is the line between normal self-exploration as a child and problematic behavior? How can I tell the difference?

Masturbation becomes a problem when it is compulsive. One of the exercises in this book will look at unmanageability. When self-stimulation controls you and you feel that you cannot stop it is out of control.

A fast way to get depressed is to violate your conscience. It may be that you have strong convictions about different issues. It may be important to you in the development of your faith to abstain from certain activities. Masturbation is definitely wrong when you are violating your own personal convictions.

When masturbation takes place in a group, with pornography, or with intense sexual fantasy, it will become harmful. Lust is specifically identified in the bible as sinful. The imagery of multiple partners that comes from habitually viewing pornography can lead to destructive consequences in relationships and marriage.

You may have become accustomed to using masturbation as a source of comfort. It may be the way you have put yourself to sleep at night. Chemicals released in the brain during orgasm cause drowsiness. It's important to develop non-sexual forms of self-comfort and anxiety management.

Most of this book will be dealing with problems connected to compulsive sexual behavior. Masturbation often falls into this category. It is not inherently evil and it is not a subject to freak out about. As we will see in principle one, shame often fuels compulsive sexual behavior. It's important to develop a healthy perspective of sexual issues based on factual information and biblical principles. Our culture teaches us about unhealthy sexuality. Learning principles of healthy sexuality is also an essential part of growth and healing.

Susan's story shows how unmanageable sexual behavior can become. The helplessness and hopelessness of being caught in an addiction can lead you to give up the fight. Maybe you've experienced the frustration of wondering why you just can't stop. You aren't acting out because of an evil heart. There are physical, emotional, and spiritual factors at work in addiction. The good news is that we have a God who heals physical, emotional, and spiritual wounds in his children. And there are ways to fight this battle that can't be done on your own. As you begin this journey of transformation, you'll come to know God like you never have before. Hope and healing may come from unexpected sources. Open yourself up to what God can do in your heart and life. Realize that we have a God who is willing to provide healing from sexual sin and addiction.

Before You Begin

You will need to have a journal to accompany this workbook. It can be as simple as a notebook with loose leaf paper or you can buy a journal just for this study. I do not recommend that you keep a journal on the computer. Ideally, write in your journal every day. This is not a diary. This is a place to write your thoughts and feelings; a place to be completely honest. If you are afraid that others will read it, keep it in a place where that is not possible. For this to be effective, you need to be able to write without editing to make it sound "right". It doesn't have to be long. Just write for about 5 or 10 minutes. Sometimes, there will be assignments in the workbook of specific things to write about. But most of the time, just write what comes up for you as you are sitting there.

Also, each day, try to identify what you are feeling. This can go in your journal. Many times young women have difficulty knowing what they are feeling. If that is true for you, use the words at the back of the book to help you. Identifying and coping with feelings is one of the core issues that you will need to deal with. So get in the habit of just taking a moment during the day and asking yourself, "What am I feeling right now?" Try to be specific. The words in the back of the workbook are in general categories which helps you to narrow it down.

Just identifying feelings is not enough. You will need to learn new coping skills to deal with what you are feeling. Sexual acting out is often a coping skill used to deal with painful emotions. So you will need to have other skills that you can use to replace it. Otherwise, it is harder to change the behavior. Some other coping skills that you might use are: listening to music; taking a walk; exercising; talking to a friend; taking a bath; reading a book; cooking; doing a hobby that you enjoy; praying; watching a funny movie; doing breathing exercises; journaling; dancing; meditating; playing with your pet; enjoying something in nature . Try to come up with a list of things that you can do to soothe yourself. Keep this list in your journal so that you will have it handy in the moments when you need it. It is harder to come up with things in the heat of the moment.

Lastly, one of the most important things that you can learn during this study is who you really are. This is the time in your life when you are supposed to be exploring and finding your identity. Spend some time looking at the material in Appendix B in the back of the book. It would be great to read through it each day if you can. Talk about it with your accountability group. You will be amazed at the difference this will make in your life when you start to believe what God says is true about you.

Congratulations! You have taken the difficult step of picking up this workbook and beginning the journey to sexual sobriety. Whether this is your first beginning, or one of many, there is hope. Other young women have found freedom using the principles in this workbook. You might feel very alone and embarrassed, afraid that no one else struggles the way that you do. Or maybe you are thinking that you don't really need help, that you can stop anytime you want to. Maybe you are discouraged because well meaning Christians have told you to just "pray more" or "have more faith". Wherever you are, please hear these words:

Welcome

You've come to the right place

You are not alonE

Principle One

We admit that we have absolutely no control of our lives. Sexual sin has become unmanageable.

Confronting Reality: I'm Shackled in My Own Prison

It started when Tina was 7. Her older brother showed her how to "touch herself" so that she would feel good. Tina tried to stop over the years but could only last a couple of weeks. Every night she would tell herself, "this is the last time." Then she would get stressed at school and do it again. Each time, she felt so ashamed and guilty. Why couldn't she stop?

Can you identify with Tina? It takes a lot of humility to admit that your life seems out of control and that sexual sin has become unmanageable. Sometimes people think that by saying their life is unmanageable they are calling themselves losers. Nothing could be further from the truth! You are precious and dearly loved, made in the image of God.

Think about the Father in the story of the prodigal son in Luke 15. He ran to meet his wayward son, watching and waiting for him to come home. The son's life was unmanageable but he was not a "loser". The Bible says that the son had to be honest with himself, to "come to his senses", before the healing could begin. That is when he could experience the love of his Father. Are you ready to come home? There is nothing that you have done that can separate you from the love of your Father. The Bible says that "nothing can separate us from the love of Christ." Do you believe that?

Assignment One: Getting Real About Sexual Truth

Let's take a moment and look at the term sexual addiction. Many young women who struggle with out of control sexual behavior would never consider themselves an addict. That is because addiction can look very different for a female than for a male. According to Patrick Carnes, sexual addiction is defined as any sexually-related, compulsive behavior which interferes with normal living and causes severe stress on family, friends, loved ones, and one's work environment. We tend to think of the male who spends hours viewing pornography on the computer or who has multiple affairs. In young women, the compulsive sexual behavior is often relational, needing to have one boyfriend after another and being sexual in order to "keep" the relationship. The goal for these women is the relationship, and sex is the means to that end. Or it can be about the romance, either real or imagined, where the high of new love is the thrill. As soon as the new wears off, she looks for another relationship in order to have the same excitement again. However, it does not have to be relational. Females compulsively masturbate and use the internet to have anonymous cybersex or visit online chat rooms in order to "hook up". We are seeing an increase in compulsive pornography use among women. Marnie Ferree in her book No Stones: Women Redeemed from Sexual Shame delineates the typical presentations of sex addiction in women. Take some time and fill out the chart next page. Remember, humility is being completely honest. That is where recovery begins.

Typical Presentations of Sexual Addiction in Women

Relationship addiction	**Began**	**How Often**
One relationship right after another (never being without a man, or at least looking for a man)		
Intense, emotional involvements, with or without sex		
Most significant relationships becoming sexual		
Simultaneous relationships, with or without sex		
Affairs (sexual or non-sexual, long term with emotional involvement, short term and non-emotional, one night stands)		

Romance addiction	**Began**	**How Often**
Fantasizing about people or relationships, real or imagined (if married, these fantasies are not about your spouse)		
Fantasizing about sexual activities, real or imagined (if married, may use fantasy to enhance sex with spouse)		
Intense, short-term relationships, with or without sex Interested in the "chase", not in maintaining a relationship		
Reading romance novels, including "Christian" ones		

Pornography and/or cybersex addiction	**Began**	**How Often**
Viewing pornography (Internet, magazines, videos, books)		
Participating in sexual chat rooms		
E-mail or cybersex relationships		
Engaging in cybersex activities		

Stereotypical "sex" addiction	**Began**	**How Often**
Compulsive masturbation, with or without pornography		
Exhibiting yourself (even if "only" through provocative clothing)		
One-night stands or sexual activity with someone you've just met (often alcohol use is a contributing factor)		
Visiting strip clubs or other voyuristic activities		
Bestiality		
Sado-masochism (S&M) or pain exchange sexual activities		

Partnering with another sex addict	**Began**	**How Often**
Choosing a sex addict for acting out partner (there may be a fine line between sex addiction and co-sex addiction)		
Selling/buying/trading sex (prostitution, stripping, using sex manipulatively to get what you want)		

Sexual anorexic	**Began**	**How Often**
Totally shut down sexually		
Compulsively avoids sex		

Your Sexual History

Sexual History

Draw a timeline of your life. One way to do this would be to write your age in the left margin of a sheet of notebook paper. Begin with your earliest memories and continue until you reach your current age. This timeline could be several pages long. In the space to the right of your age record your sexual and relationship history. The following questions can help jog your memory. They're intended to help you begin the process of telling your story. You may want to include other things that aren't listed in these questions. This can help you begin to understand how the sexual addiction started and developed over time.

1. What is your earliest memory of being sexual? How old were you? What happened? Was there anyone else involved? Did you tell anybody (parent, teacher, friend, etc…)?

2. Note the times when the frequency of sexual behaviors increased and new forms of sexual acting out began.

3. Addicts often act out when they are hungry, angry, lonely, and tired. They also act out when they are fearful, anxious, sad, and bored. Can you recognize times when these feelings prompted sexual behavior? If so, indicate on your timeline when this was true.

One of the characteristics of an addiction is that the person continues the behavior even though there are negative consequences. Sometimes the consequences are even harder to face than the behavior itself. But the reality is that our behavior does not happen in a vacuum. We impact the people around us and we impact ourselves. Take a moment and pray and ask God to help you to face and own the consequences of your sexual behavior. Then do the next exercise using the questions provided to help you.

Consequences

Consequences

Make a list of your consequences and note when they occurred on your timeline. You might want to use a different color pen for your consequences.

Physical - Have you contracted any sexually transmitted diseases like herpes, chlamydia, genital warts (HPV)? Do you need to go to a doctor or the health department to be tested for any diseases including AIDS? Have you gotten pregnant? What did you do about the pregnancy?

____

____

____

____

____

____

Emotional - What is your stress level like? Have you been losing sleep due to the guilt and shame that goes along with acting out sexually? Are you having difficulty concentrating in school? Have you been able to fulfill responsibilities at home?

____

____

____

____

____

____

____

Social - Have you been through the breakup of a dating relationship over your addiction? Are people angry with you because of things you've done to them? Have you found yourself isolating and pulling back from your relationships? Is your sexual acting out causing problems in the family with your parents or siblings? With extended family members?

____

____

____

____

____

Vocational - Perhaps you work a part time job after school. Are you using work time to be sexual? Have you lost a job due to sexual acting out on the job or with another employee?

____

____

____

____

____

Legal - Have you been arrested or spent time in jail? Have you or your family experienced any other legal consequences as a result of your sexual behavior?

____

____

____

____

____

Questions

1. Have you lied or minimized your sexual behavior in the last 6 months. Give an example.

2. Are you giving the impression that you have it all together on the outside but inside you feel confused and out of control? Give an example.

3. Many young women feel powerless in their lives and use sex as a way to feel powerful. The paradox is that when you admit that you have no power/control over the behavior you begin to get your power back. What does it mean to have no control over your life? List things over which you have no control.

Did you include your sexual behavior in the list?

____

____

4. What things **do** you have control over?

____

____

____

____

____

____

Did you include the choice to get help and do the hard work of recovery?

____

____

5. If sexual sin has become unmanageable, what things have you done in the past to try to manage the behaviors?

____

____

____

____

____

____

Recovering alcoholics often say that humility is stark raving honesty. Being completely honest with yourself and others is one of the hardest steps, yet it is crucial for recovery. Maybe you have tried to be honest with someone and they rejected you. It takes a lot of courage to try again.

Sharing your story with someone is a very important part of the healing process. This person needs to be a safe person who will love you and not use the things you tell them against you. Maybe you are doing this workbook with a mentor or youth pastor. Or maybe you are a part of a L.I.F.E. group. L.I.F.E. groups are designed to be safe places where healing can occur. There are safety guidelines for the groups but each group is responsible for following those guidelines. The important thing is that you find a place to tell your story as openly and honestly as you can. It has been said that silence keeps us sick. Breaking the silence-having a voice- is actually empowering, not diminishing like we fear. It has not been easy to do the written exercises. But now comes the hardest part. I'm pulling for you!

Assignment Two: Identifying Your Cycle of Sexual Acting Out

Have you ever thought that your out of control behavior seems to have a pattern to it? Well it does! There is a cycle that is a part of compulsive, addictive behavior. This cycle is explained in detail in Patrick Carnes' book Out of the Shadows. The good news is that by recognizing the patterns you can interrupt the sequence of behaviors. Below is Carnes' cycle of addiction.

Carnes Cycle of Addiction*

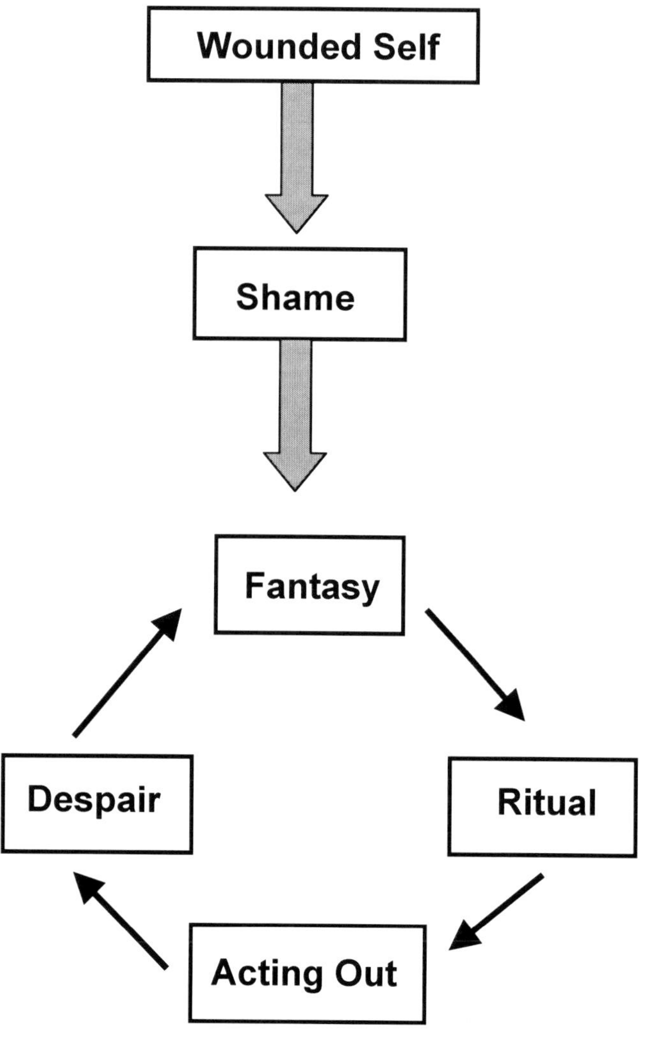

*The cycle of addiction diagram is adapted from Out of the Shadows by Dr. Patrick Carnes

Let's look at each element of the cycle and do some exercises with each one.

Wounded Self: No one grows up without wounds. These wounds can come from the culture, our peers, our experiences or our families. Some of the most damaging wounds come from abuse. In fact the research on sex addiction and abuse shows that the majority of people who struggle with sex addiction have been abused, either sexually, physically or emotionally. This abuse can come from those outside the home and those in the home. If you have been abused in any way, please get help to work through the damage. What we can do in this workbook will not be sufficient.

We live in a culture that is sexually saturated. Everything from shaving cream to chewing gum is sold using sexuality. Pornographic movies are readily available in hotels. Porn sites pop up uninvited on our computer screens. In our culture there is a strong message that women are to be sexual objects. That is how they get their worth. These underlying cultural messages as well as the constant bombardment of sexual stimuli is harmful.

Sometimes circumstances that are beyond our control can cause serious wounds. Natural disasters such as Hurricane Katrina or losing a home in a fire are examples of wounding experiences. The death of a parent or a sibling is another. Witnessing a violent event can have a profound effect on children.

We hear a lot about dysfunctional families but in truth there are no families without areas of dysfunction. So when we look at family wounds we are not talking about blame.
Abuse in the family can be overt such as sexual or physical abuse or it can be more covert and difficult to see involving emotional abuse, abandonment or neglect. In fact, the most recent research is showing that neglect does as much harm as other forms of abuse. Having rigid, inflexible rules and not much healthy touch can be very harmful to a child. The child grows up feeling abandoned and alone. Feeling like no one listens to you or that your feelings are dismissed is wounding.

Spiritual abuse is something that is not talked about very much. This can happen at church or in the home. Instead of God being presented as the loving God that He is, God is seen as judgmental and punishing. Children are made to feel guilty and ashamed for making mistakes. God is used as a reason to make children behave and "act right".

Shame: Shame is the feeling that I am defective. Wounds can cause shame, either family wounds or wounds from other people and events. The person thinks that if anyone really knew what they were like, they would reject them.

Exercise 1:

1. Think about your family. Take a piece of paper and draw a circle anywhere on the paper to represent you. Then place the members of your family where you think they belong in relationship to you on the page. Choose a shape to represent each member of the family. Include all immediate family members. Extended family and pets can be included if it seems important to you. Then draw connecting lines between the members of the family and you. These lines represent the relationship that you have with each one today. Use any code that you choose for the lines or any colors.
An example could be using a jagged line to represent a conflicted relationship where there is a lot of fighting or anger. A broken line could represent a disconnected relationship. Share your drawing with the group.

2. Fill in the blank. Put down the first words that come to mind.

Girls are

____

____

Boys are

____

____

3. What cultural messages, positive and negative, have you received about what it means to be a woman?

____

____

____

____

____

4. What feelings come up for you as you think about your family?
(Use the Feeling Words on page 109 if needed)

____

____

____

____

____

5. What events in your family were the most significant in shaping who you are?

____

____

____

____

____

____

Fantasy: The thoughts in your head about sex or the perfect guy or relationship. You can be preoccupied with these thoughts so that you are daydreaming about having sex with a certain guy or having a romantic encounter with the "guy of your dreams". Some young women are preoccupied just with having a relationship, not necessarily with a certain person. Don't all romantic relationships start this way? Yes, they often do. But it is the preoccupation with the fantasy, and using the fantasies to alter moods that is the problem.

Fantasy actually releases chemicals in the brain similar to the ones released when a person takes mood altering drugs. As with the drugs, the mood is altered in a positive direction. Where there are feelings of shame before causing a low mood, now the mood is elevated and they feel happier.

We can use our fantasies as a window into the wounds of our past. They tell us what we wish had been different about our life. Maybe you never felt special growing up but in your fantasies you are always the one who is chosen, the special one. Looking at the themes of the fantasies can be very enlightening. Often when those needs are met, the fantasies disappear.

Exercise Two:

1. What are your most common fantasies? Be specific but not graphic.

____

____

____

____

____

____

2. Is there a certain person who is in the fantasy? Is there a particular behavior? Is there a usual place that the fantasy takes place? Is it about sex or romance?

____

____

____

____

____

4. What do you see as a theme in your fantasies? What needs do you think you are trying to meet?

____

____

____

____

____

Rituals: the thoughts or behaviors that lead from fantasy or preoccupation to the acting out. Rituals can be as subtle as normal dating behavior or as obvious as going to clubs in order to pick up guys. Maybe you change your hairstyle or dress in a provocative way. Maybe you wear a special perfume or more makeup. Entering certain chat rooms can be a ritual.

Rituals begin with faulty thinking called cognitive distortions. The two most common distortions used to justify acting out are either entitlement or justification. Entitlement is thinking that you deserve a reward, that you have been "good" so you can do "just this one thing". It is thoughts of "I need to take care of myself. No one else will" or "My life is so stressful right now that I deserve this stress relief." Justification includes thoughts such as, "No one will get hurt" or "This isn't so bad. At least I am not doing…" Going along with the crowd and saying, "Everyone's doing it" is justification.

Underneath rituals are painful emotions. These emotions may be sadness, hurt, anger or loneliness. Often there is fear of abandonment, fear of rejection or fear of being alone. These painful emotions are actually driving the behavior. The rituals are an attempt to manage these emotions. It is important to note that once the ritual stage begins the acting out behavior will automatically follow. It is almost impossible to stop it from happening at this point.

Exercise 3:

1. Think about your acting out behavior. Now think back. What were you telling yourself that made it OK to go from the fantasy stage to the acting out stage? Be specific.

____

____

____

____

____

____

2. Now take what you were telling yourself and identify whether it is entitlement or justification.

____

____

____

____

____

3. What are your rituals for each acting out behavior? Be specific. Identify the feelings associated with each one. Sometimes it helps to start with the behavior and think of the steps that got to that behavior. Let's say that one form of acting out is in Internet chat rooms. Now think back to what you did before you acted out. How did you make your way to that chat room? Where did you start when you first sat down at the computer? Did you wait until everyone was asleep? Were you alone? Did you lie to anyone about who you were or what you were doing? Identify each step. They are important to stopping the behavior. It might seem trivial but put it down. Use the chart below to help. Note: One acting out behavior that is easy to overlook is being sexual with someone when you really don't want to in order to keep the relationship. This is so common for females in our society that it is easy to miss it as part of the addictive cycle.

Acting out behavior	Ritual	Feelings

Think more about this, do you see any patterns? Is there a correlation between certain behaviors and the way you were feeling?

____

____

____

____

____

Despair: This is the feeling after you have acted out. Feelings of hopelessness along with guilt and shame are common. Many people get depressed so their mood is low. How does someone elevate their low mood? They begin to fantasize and the cycle begins anew.

Now you know much more about the cycle of your particular acting out behavior. Everyone is unique so you might not fit the pattern exactly. But be careful that you are not telling yourself that you don't fit in an effort to justify your behavior. Remember, honesty is the foundation for getting well.

Assignment Three: Boundaries

Now that you know more about the cycle of addiction, what do you do with that knowledge? Insight about why you do things is not enough. The behavior needs to change. One of the ways that you can change behavior is by creating the best possible environment for success. Expecting that willpower is going to keep you from acting out, is setting yourself up for failure. Creating boundaries is the best way to set yourself up for success.

A boundary is a fence. It is a roadblock between you and your rituals. Keeping your boundaries allows you to relax and quit constantly focusing on the negative behavior. We so often focus on stopping the behavior that we cannot think of anything but that behavior. It is like telling someone to not think about chocolate. Of course they are going to think about chocolate!

Consider the behavior that you are trying to stop. What do you need to do differently so that you can succeed? If you are acting out on the computer, do you need to move it out of your room? Do you need a filter? Do you need to let someone else keep the password? These are the kinds of things that make success more of a possibility.

Use the chart below to begin making a plan to succeed. Take a moment to identify what you are feeling. Use the Feeling Words on page 109 if needed.

Ritual	Boundaries

Congratulations!

You have done a lot of hard and painful work. Think about what you have learned in Principle One- that you have no control over your life and that your sexual sin has become unmanageable. That honesty is the foundation of healing. But remember that you have a God of grace, who took care of your sin on the cross and loves to show you mercy. That will be the focus of Principle Two. I applaud your courage in continuing the journey to freedom!

We believe in God, accept the grace offered through His Son Jesus Christ, and surrender our lives and our wills to Him on a daily basis.

Finding the Solution: I Have Only One Option

Terry whispers, "I go to church and hear the sermons on sexual purity and just want to die inside. How could God love me after all I've done? It's too late for me."

Have you ever felt like Terry? Maybe you wonder if it is too late for you, if there is no going back. Or maybe you are afraid to surrender to God because you are not really sure He will love you and be there for you. He seems to take all the fun out of life and make things hard. And you are angry because He didn't protect you from pain in the past. If this is the way you feel, you are not alone.

Assignment One: Your View of God

Who is the God that you worship? Think about that for a minute. Is he like Santa Claus, knowing when you've been bad or good, so you'd better *be* good for goodness sake? Is he the kindly grandfather who is doddering and frail? Is he the cosmic vending machine that we go to when we need something? Or is he unavailable because he has more important things to do like war and poverty?

____

____

____

____

____

____

The Scripture says that God is wildly in love with you. He sings over you with delight. He sees you as his beautiful bride. And he is passionate about doing good to you and being merciful to you. Do you believe that? What you believe about God greatly impacts whether or not you can surrender to him.

Exercise

1. Your view of God can make it difficult to surrender. What is your view of God? Draw a picture of what God is like for you. Place yourself in the picture. Now think about what God was like for you when you were a little girl. Draw that picture. Is it different? How? If it is different, what happened to make it that way?

2. What is making it difficult for you to surrender to God? Are there things that you fear?

____

____

____

____

____

____

3. Do you believe that God is for you? That He will be there when you need Him? Have you felt abandoned by God in the past?

____

____

____

____

4. Sexual addiction is an attempt to feel connected and intimate. Yet it leaves a person feeling lonely and disconnected not only from people but also from God. Do a journal entry about your relationship with God. Write for 20 minutes without stopping to edit your thoughts.

Assignment Two: Cost/Benefit of Addiction and Recovery

In our culture, women are often looking for a male in authority who will rescue them or take care of them. The way to get that care is to do the right behavior. We also look at God in this same way. He will take care of me as long as I perform. And He is mad about all the wrong things that I have done.

If that is the way that you see God, then surrender to God sounds like giving control over to someone who will use and abuse you. It would make sense that you would want to maintain control under those circumstances. But in actuality, surrender to God is letting go of our need to control. It is opening our hand and releasing our lives into the good hand of a God who unconditionally loves us.

Exercise

1. Have you looked to males in authority to rescue you? Think about your relationships with guys. What have you done to try to keep them in relationship with you?

____

____

____

____

____

____

____

____

2. Do a cost/benefit analysis of your addiction. What is the payoff for you of your addiction? There is always a payoff or we would not keep doing the behavior. It might be helpful to think about the last time you were in a relationship or you sexually acted out. What do you think you were getting out of it?

____

____

____

____

Now think about the cost to you of continuing your addiction. What are the costs?

____

____

____

____

3. What are the costs of recovery? What would you have to change or give up? Take some time here. It is hard to fully embrace recovery if you do not know what the costs are.

____

____

____

____

What are the benefits of giving up your addiction?

____

____

____

Assignment Three: Grieving Losses

Grace means that God has forgiven all my sin. That means that God is not bent out of shape about my sin. That might be shocking to you but that is what grace means. He has forgiven my sin, past, present and future. That is not to say that He does not care about my sin. He cares deeply about my sin because it keeps me from experiencing all that He has for me, the abundant life that He promised.

If grace was only forgiveness of sins, that would be wonderful. But it is so much more. The Bible says that I am righteous. What does that mean? Think about your bank account for a moment. Let's say you forget your balance and keep spending money. The bank sends you overdraft notices and now you are even more overdrawn. You go to the bank and try to work something out. They agree to forgive the overdraft charges and you are delighted that you are back up to a zero balance. That is forgiveness and it is wonderful. But what if the bank put a million dollars into your account? Now that is absolutely incredible and you would be dancing for joy. That is what righteousness is. God's riches are put in my account. Now that is good news! I am not just forgiven, I am righteous. I am a new creation. I now can surrender to God and have power over sin.

Exercise:

1. Often women who struggle with sex addiction fear abandonment and being alone. They fear that no one will want them. Have you felt abandoned and rejected by people who were important to you? Maybe you weren't actually abandoned but you still felt it. Who were they? What feelings come up for you as you think about these people? Try to be specific about the feelings. Use the feeling chart at the back of the book. Note: This can be very hard to look at and can bring up powerful feelings of sadness. Hang in there. It takes time to process these feelings. But you will get to the other side.

____

____

____

____

2. What did you tell yourself about who you were after the abandonment or rejection?

____

____

____

____

____

____

3. Think about what God says about you, that you are dearly loved, forgiven and righteous. If you believed it, what difference would it make in how you see yourself? What changes would it make in your life? Be specific.

____

____

____

____

____

____

4. Grieving is going to be a large part of recovery. And grieving is about acknowledging pain, something that we are very good at avoiding. In fact, sexual acting out is an attempt to manage painful feelings. Make a list of the cost to you of your addiction. Now add the cost to you of the rejection and abandonment that you felt, even if you weren't truly abandoned but just felt it. What were the costs to you of growing up in the home that you did? Of attending the church or school that you attended? Think about the losses that you have experienced. This is not about blame. It is about acknowledging the pain. Use the chart below to help.

Losses

Addiction Home School Church Other

____

____

____

____

____

____

____

____

____

Take a moment to identify what you are feeling. Use the Feeling Words on page 109 if needed.

Principle Three

We courageously make a list of all of our sins and weaknesses and confess those to a person of spiritual authority.

Telling the Truth: I Must Leave the Darkness.

"I know I need to talk to somebody. But I'm afraid to tell the truth. In my Bible study one girl asked for prayer because she felt so guilty that she was kissing her boyfriend. How am I going to tell them that I am sleeping with mine?"

In Principle One we began being honest about our sexual sin. In Principle Two, we saw that our only option was to surrender control to God who forgives our sin and restores and transforms our lives. In Principle Three, we will courageously face up to our sins and confess them to a trustworthy person.

It is hard to face the truth about ourselves, much less share it with another person. We fear rejection and isolation. "If they really knew me, they would reject me," is what we tend to believe. So we lie to cover up what we have done and who we really are. Instead of getting the connection and intimacy that our hearts long for, we get more isolation and disconnection, the very things we are trying to avoid by not telling the truth. It is a paradox, that when we are completely honest with people and they know us for who we really are, then we can develop intimate, close relationships with God and each other. We can be our true selves and stop pretending.

Assignment One: Examining Our Relationships

One of the ways that we get a sense of who we are is in relationship with others. Think about your friendships and relationships. What are they like? Can you be honest or do you have to pretend to be someone that you are not? Do you feel supported and loved, empowered to be the best person that you can be, or do you feel devalued and diminished as a person? What is your communication like? Do you have to lie to protect your image? Do they send you positive or negative messages about who you are? Safe people allow you to be who you are and think the best of you. Safe people keep the confidences that you share so you can be honest with them.

On a blank sheet of paper, draw what is called a social atom. Use symbols to represent all the significant people in your life including yourself. Draw the symbol for yourself on the page anywhere that seems appropriate to you. Locate the other significant people in your life anywhere that seems right on the page in relationship to you. Then draw lines of communication between you and the other people in your life. Represent what that communication is like with the line that you draw. An example might be a broken line if the communication is not good. Or it might be a jagged line if it is conflictual.

What conclusions do you draw about the relationships in your life? Your family? Your friends? Boys? Are there people that are safe? Who are they? Are there people that are unsafe? Who are they? What conclusions are you drawing about yourself from the people in your life?

____

____

____

____

____

____

Assignment Two: Exposing the Darkness

This is going to be one of the most painful assignments. Take your time and think back over your life. Make a list of all the things that you have done that you are ashamed of. Include your sexual acting out. Also include thoughts and beliefs that you think are wrong. Some of the items will be the same as the timeline. But this will include more than your sexual behavior.

One of the most important things to look at is lying. Somewhere along the line, you began to tell lies about your behavior. When we fear being known, we have to tell lies to cover up who we are and what we have done. Someone has said that every addiction is a double addiction, one to the substance or experience and one to lying. What lies have you told yourself about your behavior? What lies have you told others to protect yourself? Ask God to help you. This assignment is not to increase your sense of shame, but to help you to get free from shame. Things that are not brought into the light and acknowledged have power over us.

It might be helpful to think of your life in segments, early childhood, childhood and adolescence. This will be a long assignment. Sometimes it helps to do it in several sittings. Don't think about sharing this right now. You can make a choice about that later. Just do this for *you* at this time.

Questions to ask before beginning the list

1. What thoughts do you have when you think about making this list? What feelings?

____

____

____

____

____

____

2. Are there legitimate concerns that you have? What can you do about them?

____

____

____

____

____

____

3. Think for a moment about the people who you do not want to know about your acting out. Your parents might be on this list. What do you fear? Facing your fear is one of the hardest things that you will have to do. What will you lose if these people find out? What will it cost you to stay silent? List these people and by each name write what you fear will happen if they know.

____

____

____

____

____

____

Assignment Three: Confessing The Darkness

The Bible says in James 5:16 that we are to "confess our sins one to another so that we might be healed." It is important to note that the purpose of confessing our sins is healing; it is not to cause more harm. Many times we fear confession because we fear rejection and alienation. But telling the truth about what we have done is a way to get free. Remember…addiction flourishes in the isolation of silence. Telling our story can give us new insight into how to behave differently in the future. We can receive forgiveness and more self acceptance. Often we find out that we are not the only ones who have thought and done the things we are relating.

In Assignment One of Principle Three, you identified the safe people in your life. Think for a moment about a safe person that you will be able to share your list with from Assignment Two. Preferably, it will be a safe adult, such as your sponsor or youth pastor.
According to Stephanie Covington, there are several questions to consider when choosing someone to hear your confession.

- Do they have an understanding of what you are trying to accomplish?
- Do they respect your privacy and confidentiality?
- Can they listen attentively?
- Do they have the ability to be emotionally present when you express pain?
- Do they have the ability to hear what you say without being personally hurt by it?

And I would add one more:

- Do they have your best interest at heart?

Now, take some time and pray and ask God to show you who to ask to hear your confession. Search your heart and think about the motive for choosing that person and for making your confession. Some questions to consider from Mark Laaser:

- Are you confessing out of a desire to manipulate to get someone's forgiveness?
- Do you think this is a one time event and you will not have to confess again?
- Are you just trying to get the assignment over with?
- Are you trying to keep people pleased with you by confessing?

- Do you have a repentant heart and a humble attitude? Pray and ask God to give you a brokenness that leads to repentance. Caution: If you wait until your heart is perfectly right, you may never take this step.
-

If you have answered the questions above and you are ready to talk to the safe person that you have chosen, then there are some guidelines around the disclosure itself. There could be other people who you have harmed with your behavior who could be harmed again by your disclosure. Be sensitive to that as you share. You might want to ask forgiveness of someone who you have acted out with. If this is the case, take a safe third person with you instead of doing that alone. Also, other people do not need to hear every detail of your acting out. You need to be honest and to tell the whole story, but you do not need to give graphic details.

Exercise:

You are ready to share your story now. The first person to share your story with is God. He wants to hear your confession so that you can be free. He loves to forgive you because that is His nature. God says in 1 John 1:9, "If we confess our sins He is faithful and just to forgive us our sins and to cleanse us from all unrighteousness." When you think about it, confession turns you back to God, rather than away from Him. That delights His heart. Do you think that God is disillusioned with you? He never had any illusions about you! He understands that you are human and He is wildly in love with you. Receive His forgiveness right now.

Now share your story with the person that you have chosen. When you are finished, write in your journal about the experience. Be sure to include feeling words. What was it like to have to set up the appointment? To begin to talk? After you finished? Later that day or night? How do you feel now? What do you wish that you had known before you started? Was it like you expected?

____

____

____

____

Note: If you are feeling shame and condemnation after your disclosure, look up 1 John 3:20 which says, "If our hearts condemn us, God is greater than our hearts." Go to Him and ask Him to help you. He is ready and willing to come to your aid.

Take a moment to identify what you are feeling. Use the Feeling Words on page 109 if needed.

Principle Four

We seek accountability and to build our character as children of God.

Growing in Transformation: I Mature in Character

Lauren sighed and said, "No one else struggles the way that I do. I try and try but can't seem to stop looking at pornography on the Internet. I talked to my Sunday school teacher and she wants me to join a group at church. I'm not going to go to a group where they tell you what you can and can't do. I'm not like those other people. I just haven't found what works for me yet."

Have you ever felt this way? Do you squirm when you think about people telling you what to do? Do you believe that you are a special case? The word accountability can have a negative connotation. It makes us think of being controlled and restricted, not free to be who we are. However, real accountability actually helps us to be our best selves. We can share our struggles and have people who love and care about us walk alongside. It is important to have people who are more mature in the faith to help us. We all have blind spots that others can help us see.

God made us to be in relationship with other people. When you think about Adam and Eve before the Fall, they were "naked and unashamed." They were able to be vulnerable and honest with each other. They began to hide and to cover themselves *after* they sinned. And we are still doing that today. Our sin makes us want to hide. Yet our design is to be in a community where we can expose our weaknesses and let the other parts of the body help us. We can stop pretending and hiding and have real intimacy. As we tell other people what we are really like, they can help us develop our character so that we become all that we were designed to be.

Assignment One: Accepting The Need For Accountability

There are two kinds of accountability that you need to have. One is with a mentor, a woman who is farther along, older and wiser, who can help hold you accountable for your choices. As a younger woman, it helps to have an older woman who can walk with you and help you stay on the journey of faith. This mentor can be a college woman if you are in high school. She can be a young mother or career woman if you are in college. Think about women at your church or family members. It just needs to be an older woman who you respect and look up to. Recently a young friend was hospitalized with an eating disorder. Before she went in, I told her to remember my face when she was tempted to lie about what she was eating. She later said that it was that accountability that kept her honest about her food. Just knowing that there will be someone who will ask you the hard questions will empower you to make choices that you have been unable to make on your own.

We have been talking about the characteristics of safe people. A mentor needs to have those traits. A mentor needs to be someone who is dependable and consistent. They need to understand the time and availability commitment. You would need someone who can commit to regularly talking and meeting with you. A mentor is someone who is not afraid to speak the truth but does so in love. They want the best for you and believe in you. They see your potential and encourage you to continue on the journey of recovery. This person can give you hope on the days when you are feeling hopeless. But this person also confronts you when it is necessary.

Many times young women who are sexually acting out do not have a good relationship with one or both of their parents. They feel emotionally or physically abandoned in some way. As we have seen from the cycle of addiction, young women act out in an attempt to medicate the pain of those wounds. You probably will be uncomfortable letting someone in and being responsible to tell them what is really going on in your life. Remember, people who struggle with addictions are more comfortable isolating and not having genuine connection with anyone. This is a part of the process of learning to be truly intimate.

There is a truism that when you are wounded in relationship, you need to get healed in relationship. The bond with your mentor can be a nurturing connection that helps to heal the wounds of the past. Think about the Bible story of Ruth and Naomi. When Ruth's husband died, Naomi told her that she could go back to her own people. But Ruth passionately said that she would stay with Naomi and that Naomi's people would become her family. Naomi must have loved Ruth in such a way that Ruth preferred to stay with her rather than go back to her own family.

Some questions to ask as you consider a mentor:

- Can you trust this person to be confidential?
- Can this woman help you make a plan to keep you from sexually acting out?
- Can this person confront you when necessary?
- Can you share past sins and current struggles with this person without judgment?
- Can this woman hold you accountable?
- Do you respect this woman?
- Is this person encouraging?
- Does this woman understand about sexual addiction or do you think that she would be willing to learn?

Now write down the names of women that you would consider asking to be a mentor. Pray and ask God to lead you to the woman that would be best for you. Talk with the one that you decide on. Make sure that she understands the commitment and what you want her to do. Be specific. Plan your first meeting time. Keep a record of what you are learning in your journal.

Marnie Ferree has a list of accountability questions. You and your mentor can create a list that would be appropriate for you.

1. Is there anything that is bothering you?
2. Did you violate any boundaries?
3. Did you have any painful or strong feelings today?
4. Did you do any behaviors today that were used to medicate painful feelings?
5. Did you fantasize?

6. Have you masturbated?
7. Have you been on any inappropriate Internet sites?
8. Has there been any provocative behavior?
9. Have you taken care of yourself physically? How much sleep did you get last night?
10. How much TV have you watched?
11. Have you been limiting what you eat? Compulsively eating? Compulsively exercising? Compulsively shopping?
12. Have you been flirting or using sexual humor?
13. Are there any specific areas where you need accountability?
14. Have you told any lies?
15. Have you fully disclosed everything?

Is there anything else that you would add?

____

____

____

____

____

____

Healthy Choices

You also want to be accountable for doing positive behaviors that are good for you and build your character. Some of these are:

1. prayer
2. Bible study
3. service to others
4. caring for your health
5. playing

6. eating healthy foods
7. resting
8. connecting with safe people
9. journaling
10. meditating
11. practicing gratitude
12. managing money well
13. using good study habits

What other positive behaviors can you add?

____

____

____

____

____

Accountability Groups

The other type of accountability that you will need to have is an accountability group of your peers. It is important to learn to be real with a group of young women who struggle just like you do. You have been pretending to be someone that you are not. This is a place to practice the new behavior of being your real self. We are made to be relational. This is a place to have a group of people who you can be truly intimate with. They will love you as you really are and tell you the truth. They will not let you get away with lying to yourself and others because that is not what is best for you. This group needs to know your particular pattern of acting out, your triggers and rituals. This is so that they can help you if you are deceiving yourself about your behavior. The best people to help you see your dishonesty are other people who struggle with the same thing.

Anytime someone decides to get help with an addiction, they often lose most of their friends. These are the people they acted out with or they go to places they do not want to go anymore. One young man told me that he got sober from alcohol and then had nowhere to go and no friends to do anything with. His life had organized around alcohol and his friends all partied and went to bars. Until he started a recovery group, he went to the bars with his friends and just didn't drink. How long do you think it was before he had a relapse?

You also are going to have time on your hands that used to be spent acting out. Your accountability group is a place to make new friends and to have somewhere to go that is safe. The group can help fill the time that used to be spent acting out. Along with meeting together, you can eat as a group or do service projects. Be creative about opportunities to get together.

In your group, you can use the same list of questions that are listed above to use with your mentor. The positive behaviors that you are doing to replace the negative ones are very important. So check on the healthy choices each time. Talk about the ones that are hard for you. What makes it hard? Where have you seen improvement? Be sure that you each do a feelings check at every meeting. Learning to identify your feelings and label them is a very important tool for recovery.

Assignment Two: Being True To Ourselves

A very important part of maturing in character for females is learning to have a voice. Our voice is the way that we tell others who we really are. Each of us has a true self that is amazingly unique, created in God's image. You have hopes, dreams, aspirations, gifts, longings, thoughts, feelings, experiences, personality, character and beliefs that make up who you are. Do you believe the Scripture that says that you are "wonderfully made"? Many times through things that have been done to us or choices that we have made, we can lose touch with our authentic self and act out of a false self, pretending to be someone that we are not. We play a role, hiding our true selves and only showing others what we think they will like. Many times girls actually change their opinions and become whatever the person wants them to be. Can you relate to being a chameleon, changing how you appear in order to blend in?

Questions to Consider

1. When you think about letting people know who you really are, what feelings come up for you? Why?

____

____

____

____

____

2. Are there situations and certain types of people where you are more prone to hide? Who or what are they?

____

____

____

____

____

3. Do you know what your true self is like? Who are you? Describe yourself. Include the categories listed above i.e. hopes, dreams, characteristics, personality, etc. It might help to fill in the blank: I am a person who…

Note: Many times we are afraid to describe ourselves in positive ways. Sometimes it helps to think about yourself as a little girl. What were you like? You have changed, but many of the traits you had then, you have now.

____

____

____

____

____

____

4. Did you have trouble with question 3? If yes, why did you?

____

____

____

____

____

____

Assignment Three: Maturing In Character

Principle Four focuses on maturing in character. One way we do this is with accountability. Another is by learning to know who we are and to act consistently out of our true self. Now we will look at character itself. Character is often described as who you are when no one is watching. It is the collection of attributes that help you make moral and ethical choices. A woman of good character makes choices consistent with her beliefs and values. Traits like honesty, integrity, caring, responsibility and trustworthiness are all a part of character.

Character is not something that you are born with. It is something that develops. That is good news! That means that we are not stuck in old patterns of behavior. We can change. We can make choices to build our character based on what God says in His Word. In 2 Peter 1: 5-8 (The Message) God says, " So don't lose a minute in building on what you've been given, complementing your basic faith with good character, spiritual understanding, alert discipline, passionate patience, reverent wonder, warm friendliness, and generous love, each dimension fitting into and developing the others. With these qualities active and growing in your lives, no grass will grow under your feet, no day will pass without its reward as you mature in your experience of our Master Jesus."

According to these verses, good character and the other six traits are built onto our basic faith. They also "fit into and develop each other". So as you work on developing your character, you impact your spiritual understanding and vice versa. As you develop self discipline it impacts your character and vice versa. This might be somewhat overwhelming as you think about where you are in your character development and where you want to be. Remember, it is God who works in you. He will be your strength as you make these changes. Galatians 3: 5 (the Message) says, " Answer this question: Does the God who lavishly provides you with his own presence, his Holy Spirit, working things in your lives you could never do for yourselves, does he do these things because of your strenuous moral striving *or* because you trust him to do them in you?" You don't need to try harder or white knuckle your character development. Just keep giving yourself back to God for Him to change you and continue to make decisions consistent with who you want to be.

Questions

1. What traits make up character? Give an example of someone who has this trait for each trait listed. It can be someone you know or someone famous, either alive today or historical.

____

____

____

____

____

____

2. Which are your character strengths and which do you need to work on?

____

____

____

____

____

____

3. Since the Scripture says that there are 6 traits that also work together with character to help with its development, give a definition and a reasonable goal for each of them. Remember, it is God who works this out in you. You participate to be sure, but the Holy Spirit is the one who empowers the change. Pray and ask Him to help you to believe that He will do it.

Spiritual understanding

Definition:____

____

Goal:____

____

Alert Discipline

Definition:____

____

Goal:____

____

Passionate Patience

Definition:____

____

Goal:____

____

Reverent Wonder

Defintion:____

____

Goal:____

____

Warm Friendliness

Definition:____

____

Goal:____

____

Generous Love

Definition:____

____

Goal:____

____

Remember, real love wants what is best for another person, affirms and empowers that person. In the next section we will look at ways we have not loved others well and further develop our character as we take responsibility for our actions.

Take a moment to identify what you are feeling. Use the Feeling Words on page 109 if needed.

Principle Five

We explore the damage we have done, accept responsibility, and make amends for our wrongs.

Demonstrating Real Change: I Accept Responsibility

"My little sister is starting to follow in my footsteps," Lauren said. "I never thought about how my behavior would affect her. How can I tell her not to do these things when I did them? I'd give anything to stop her from having to feel the pain that I feel."

We are making a transition now in the focus of the work in this guide. Up until now, the work has been mainly self focused. Let's briefly review the first principles. You have taken a sincere look at your sexual sin, admitted that you were powerless and that your behavior had become unmanageable. Surrendering to God on a daily basis you began the process of forgiveness. You have made a list of your sins and confessed them to another person. And you have begun to develop godly character.

Now the work is going to become more others focused. You will still be looking at yourself but we are going to expand our vision and include other people. One of the difficult realizations when people are going through recovery is the impact of their out of control behavior on other people. Some of the impact you are probably well aware of and might like to forget. But there could be damage that you might not have thought about before.

The purpose of looking at the hurt and pain that your behavior has caused other people is not to create more shame. It is so that you can begin to take responsibility for your actions and to make amends. We will look at making amends in more detail in a later assignment. Please give yourself grace as you begin to assess the harm that your sexual behavior has caused other people. Taking responsibility is for your healing, not to bring you harm.

Assignment One: Accessing The Damage

In this assignment you will begin making a list of the people that you have harmed as a result of your addiction. Remember, this is to help you develop your character NOT to create more shame. Accepting responsibility and making amends brings freedom. Creating shame does not. If you begin to feel shame, discuss how you are feeling with your accountability partners.

It might be helpful to consider categories of harm when making your list. People can be harmed emotionally, physically, spiritually and financially. Perhaps you can think of other ways that people have been affected by your actions. You might want to start with a list of no more than 10 people. Then add people as you think of them. This is not a one time event. As in making your sexual history, you might need to come back to this many times as God brings people and hurts to mind.

Think about family, friends, coworkers, employers, pastors and teachers. Some questions to consider that might spark your memory.

- Did you lie to anyone in the course of your acting out?
- Did you violate anyone's trust?
- Did you use another person when you acted out?
- Did you steal anything?
- Did you abuse computer privileges at home, school or work?
- Did you give a sexually transmitted disease to anyone?
- Did you cheat on anyone?
- Did you talk about girlfriends in dishonest ways?
- Did you perform poorly at work as a result of your acting out?

Now pray and ask God to help you to be honest and to give you grace to accept responsibility for your actions. Ask Him to remind you of people who need to be on the list. Remember- no shame! If this gets emotionally draining, take a break and do something soothing like listening to music or taking a walk.

Next to the name, put the harm that happened to them as a result of your behavior. Do not take responsibility for things that they did. Just look at what you are responsible for. Try to put yourself in their shoes so that you can understand what it felt like for them. The possible feelings they had will be an important part of the process. Sometimes it helps to think about the person sitting across from you in a chair. Imagine switching places with them. Now what might they say they felt when this occurred?

Next, think about what was going on in you when each thing happened. What were you feeling? What character qualities were you displaying? Was there anger, pride, sadness, selfishness? Was something painful happening in your life at the time that was overwhelming? Include this next to each name and event.

Remember, take your time and be gentle with yourself. God promises forgiveness. We just need to change our thinking about what we did, which is what repentance means. You are in the process of changing your thinking.

Assignment Two: Preparing To Make Amends

Now that you have made a list of the people that have been harmed by your behavior, it is time to think about making amends. Remember the story of Zaccheus? He wanted to pay back several times what he had stolen from the people in tax money. It is important to make restitution where you are able to do so, to make what is called amends. Making amends involves going to each person on your list and telling them you are sorry for each thing that you have done that has caused them harm. Be specific but not graphic. Remember how you thought about what it probably felt like for them? This would be a good time to say something like, "I would imagine that you felt betrayed," or "If it had happened to me, I would have felt hurt." Whatever you thought they might be feeling could be included here. Be remorseful with no expectation of forgiveness. This is about you taking ownership of what you have done, not seeking something from them. Then, if there is restitution to be made, this is the time to do it.

Sometimes it is not possible to make restitution. Either the person is no longer living or you do not know where they are or it would be harmful to them or to you to make amends. In those instances you can make indirect amends. Indirect amends can be contributions made in the name of the person or a service that you do for others that only you know is done in that person's honor as a way to make restitution. Be creative. There are many ways to make indirect amends. But whenever possible, make direct amends. If you have questions about the appropriateness of direct or indirect amends, talk it over with your sponsor or accountability partner.

It is important to check your attitude and motive for making amends. Some motives are more about you wanting to receive something from the person you have harmed rather than you giving something to them. Some unhealthy reasons for apologizing are:

- Wanting to get someone to quit being angry with you
- Wanting to reestablish contact with an old partner
- Wanting to get over your guilt feelings
- Trying to control a relationship
- Trying to keep from being abandoned in a relationship
- Trying to get them to apologize for what they have done

- Wanting to tell them how angry you are in the form of an apology
- Trying to avoid consequences for what you have done

Healthy motives would be:

- Having empathy for the harm that you have caused another person
- Wanting to accept responsibility for what you have done
- Wanting to make restitution for the harm

Now next to each name in the list that you have made, include your motive for making amends. Be honest. Are any of your motives unhealthy? What do you need to do differently? What might be keeping you from making amends? When you think about making amends, what feelings come up for you?

Remember, when you are making amends, the only person that you can control is you. So do not look for a response from them. They might be too angry to truly listen to you. Reconciliation of relationship would be great, but it cannot be a goal for your amends. Let go of a desire to control the outcome and have it be a certain way. Ask God to help you to be truly repentant and humble as you talk to the people on your list. They will sense any defensiveness. Watch for "I'm sorry but…" The word "but" after the words "I'm sorry" cancels out the apology. That is making excuses.

Now make a plan. Who will you approach first? What amends will you make? Talk to your accountability partners before beginning to make amends. Get feedback. Are there people who they think are missing from your list that need to be there? Do they see any unhealthy motives? Do they agree with your plan? When will you start? Pray and ask God to guide you and to give you courage to begin.

____

____

____

____

____

Assignment Three: Making Amends

Now it is time to put your plan into action. This often is one of the most difficult assignments. But the good news is that it can be one of the most freeing and rewarding. You will want to make direct amends where it is possible to do so. Make indirect amends where it is not safe to make direct amends or where it is impossible to do so, such as the person is no longer living. Remember that you have no control over how the other person responds. Your goal is just to tell them that you are sorry for what you have done. You want to do what is right regardless of the other person's response.

It is important that you prayerfully prepare for making amends. How are you feeling when you think about talking to the people on your list? Journal about those feelings. Ask God to help you. Role play what you will say with your accountability partners. Get feedback. Prepare for how you will respond if they do not welcome you. That will help you to have more confidence in your ability to communicate. Spend time meditating on Matthew 22:37-40. Jesus says this sums up all we should be doing as followers of Him. What does this have to do with your amends? Journal your answer.

Direct Amends:

There are some guidelines for making direct amends that are important to consider.

- Direct amends need to happen in person, face to face. Consider each person and how you can accomplish that. Will you call them, write or e-mail to set up a time and place? Bend over backwards to accommodate them.
- Be clear and upfront about your reason for wanting to talk to them. Tell them that you want to apologize for the harm you have done. They might be wary about talking to you at all. Remember, you have hurt them. Some people will want to just talk to you on the phone and not meet. That probably feels less threatening to you too. But it is better for both of you if you can apologize in person. Sometimes a third person such as your mentor is needed to facilitate a meeting.
- Be clear about the harm that you have done. Do not make excuses or bring up things that they have done to hurt you. Be specific about what you are apologizing for. For example say, "I'm sorry that I lied to you about having the profile on the internet. I betrayed your trust and that must have really hurt." Don't be vague and just say, "I'm sorry that I hurt you."
- Be clear about what you intend to do differently. This is the place to share your plan to make restitution if that is needed. Think through what you would need to do to make the relationship better.
- Listen to them as they respond to your apology. Do not be defensive in your response to them. Give them space to be angry or distrustful of you. Remember, you have no control over their reaction. You are just trying to do the right thing. There will be moments that are uncomfortable.
- Go without expectations. You are just taking responsibility for your actions. You are not looking for forgiveness. If they offer it that will be great. But do not go expecting it. Some people will welcome you. Others will not want to listen to you. Their response is not the goal.

- Thank them for listening to you. Be appreciative of the time that they took to meet with you. Thank them for sharing their feelings.

Indirect amends:

There are times that it is not safe or it is not possible to make direct amends. That is when you will need to make indirect amends. It might not be safe for you to sit down with a former sexual partner and make amends. Or the person you need to make amends to is no longer living, or you do not know where they are. Sometimes the people you have acted out with are anonymous and you need to make symbolic or indirect amends. There are many ways to make indirect amends. Some suggestions are:

- Volunteer with an organization that teaches about sexual purity and the dangers of pornography
- Be involved with school groups promoting abstinence
- Help with youth church
- Teach young girls in Sunday school or VBS
- Keep yourself sexually pure. Maintain your own sobriety. Use your sobriety as a memorial to honor those you have acted out with.
- Treat others as you would want to be treated. Practice the Golden Rule.

Be creative. There are limitless ways that you can symbolically make amends to someone that you have harmed. Ask God to help you with ideas.

____

____

____

____

____

So far in Principle Five, you have taken responsibility for your actions by making amends to others for what you have done. Now you are going to take responsibility by forgiving others for the harm that they have done. This can be a painful assignment. It requires you to remember things that you might have wanted to forget. Some of you have undoubtedly experienced great harm from other people in your life. There are some things that you need to know about forgiveness before you start.

- Forgiveness is a process. It can be a one time event but often is not. Just be willing to enter into the process. God will help you along. In the future, when you remember those hurtful events, just remind yourself that you have already chosen to forgive and pray and bless that person.

- Forgiveness does not mean that what the person did doesn't matter. It means that you are giving up the right to get even.
- Forgiveness is not the same as reconciliation. You can forgive even if the person never acknowledges that they were wrong. Reconciliation means that the person admits that they were wrong and wants to be reconciled with you.
- Forgiveness does not mean forgetting. Some things you will not remember over time. But other things you will not ever forget.
- Forgiveness is a choice. It is a choice for your healing. When you hold grudges, you become bitter and critical. Choosing to forgive is a choice for your freedom.

Exercise:

Meditate on Ephesians 4:32. Think about God's forgiveness of you. Journal your thanksgiving to God. Now think about the people who you need to forgive. Is there something making it hard to forgive? Pray and ask God to help you. Make a list of the people and the hurts that you need to forgive. This is one of those assignments that you might need to continue to come back to again and again. Now make the choice to forgive the people who have harmed you. Sometimes all we can do is to ask God to make us willing to forgive them. If that is where you are with some of the people, then give yourself grace. You are willing to enter the process. God promises to help you. Share with your group or your mentor about the hurts that you have chosen to forgive. Ask them to pray with you. You might enjoy a ritual that will help cement the choice in your mind. You can write the things you have forgiven on pieces of paper and burn them. Or you can nail them to a cross, symbolically giving them to Jesus. Some groups have done an exercise together where each person put the hurts they were forgiving in their own helium balloon and they released the balloons together. You might want to light a candle and name the hurts out loud and then say, "I choose to forgive."

You have come a long way in your journey of recovery. Take a moment and savor how far you have come. Congratulations for continuing in the process!

Take a moment to identify what you are feeling. Use the Feeling Words on page 109 if needed.

Principle Six

In fellowship with others we develop honest, intimate relationships where we celebrate our progress and continue to address our weaknesses.

Living in Fellowship: I Cannot Succeed Alone

"I was scared at first to share all the things that I had done," writes Sarah. "But after I saw how much support I got from the other girls in my group, I wish that I had done it sooner. It helps me to stay sober when I know that the others are there for me. When I am tempted to act out, I remember that they are pulling for me and I call one of them to help me. I wouldn't make it without them."

Sexual addiction is by definition an intimacy disorder. It is trying to get connection and relationship in a way that just makes you feel more isolated. How many times have you wanted to stay away from other people because of the secrets that you carried? This shame keeps you from connecting with other people and having real relationships. Then the lack of connection and isolation drives the addiction and on it goes in the cycle.

It is difficult if not impossible to stay sober in isolation. You need other people to help you in the journey of recovery. God made us relational. He intends for us to help and encourage one another. It is much easier to remain sexually pure when we have other people who are walking with us on our journey. We need other people to hold us accountable and to love us when we mess up. There is something about the support of others who are fellow strugglers which spurs us on to make lasting change.

So far you have had to tell your story to others and begin to trust them with your secrets. You have taken major steps out of shame and isolation. You have taken the risky step of letting people see who you really are, the basis of intimate relationship. Hopefully, you are feeling more connected and intimate with at least one other person. I John 1:7 says, "If we walk in the light as He is in the light we have fellowship with one another and the blood of Jesus Christ His Son cleanses us from all sin." What a wonderful promise. As you walk in the light with God, you will have intimate connection with other people. The starting place is a heart connection with God where we know that our sins are forgiven. Out of that connection with God, flows a heart connection with people that can be open and honest.

Assignment One: Practicing Meditation

Many times the focus of recovery is on stopping certain behaviors. And this is right. At first, the focus needs to be on stopping the behavior that is unmanageable and out of control. But this necessary part of the recovery process can send a false message that behavior is the most important thing. In truth, God wants your heart *and* your behavior. Sexual integrity will flow out of a heart that is transformed. In Matthew 22: 38-40, Jesus is asked what the greatest commandment is. He says, "You shall love the Lord your God with all your heart, and with all your soul, and with all your mind. And a second is like it: You shall love your neighbor as yourself." He then goes on to say that all the Law and Prophets hang on these two commands. In other words, all right behaviors come from these two commands. And they are about the heart. They are about loving God, your neighbor and yourself.

The Bible says that we love God because He first loved us. When we know and accept how much He loves us, we love Him back. And we can't really love others or ourselves and have intimate, honest relationships until we truly know how much He loves us. Do you believe that God loves you? Of course, you say. But do you really? Does He like you? Is He crazy about you? God doesn't love you any more when you are sober than He does when you are acting out. You can't do anything or be anything to make Him love you more. And you can't do anything or be anything to make Him love you less. When you come to Christ in salvation, your sin is taken care of; it is paid for on the cross by Jesus. Do you believe this? That is the outrageous good news of the gospel. His grace seems too good to be true.

What is God like? You might have a difficult time thinking about God as loving because of experiences that you have had in your life. Or maybe you cannot relate to God as Father because you did not have an earthly father who was good to you. The thought of God as Father makes you think of harshness and pain. Or maybe your father was distant and uninvolved so God seems that way too. Or maybe you think God is disappointed in you because of your sexual sin.

The Bible says that God is full of love and compassion. It says that He is a God of peace and rest who wants to take all your heavy burdens and make them light for you. He sings over you and will never, ever forget you. His heart is so full of love for you that He has a pet name for you that only He knows. He was the one who made you in your mother's womb and knitted you together just the way you are because He loved you that way. You are special to Him. He is forgiving and gracious and overflowing with joy. He promises to help you when you need help. And He says that He will shelter and protect you under His outstretched arms. Wow! What a God we have!

Exercises:

1. What is God like for you? Take out your journal and pray and ask God to show Himself to you. Then journal about who God is to you.

____

____

____

____

____

____

2. Research is showing that meditation actually changes the chemistry of the brain making it more stable and functional. We are going to practice meditation. Hopefully, you will enjoy meditation and it will become a part of your relationship with God. Pick your favorite Bible story. Now I want you to think about it in a certain way. Go to a place where you can be quiet and undisturbed. Read your favorite story several times very slowly. Let the words wash over you.

Now stop and meditate on these verses.

Answer the questions below before you go on.

1. Did any part of the passage really jump out at you? What was it? Was it a word or phrase or something that you noticed for the first time?

____

____

____

____

____

____

2. What are you feeling as you think about the story? Are there any memories that are coming up for you? Write them down.

____

____

____

____

____

____

3. What is God like in the passage?

___

___

___

___

___

___

Now close your eyes and say very slowly and calmly, something like Jesus, I belong to you; or maybe just the word, stillness. Whatever works for you to help you quiet your heart. You should notice that your breathing gets slower and your heart rate slows down. Now imagine yourself in the story that you just read. If it is a story that takes place outside, imagine that you are there. Is it hot or windy? Where is God? Where are you? If Jesus is in your story, look at His face. How would you describe Him? Does He look at you? What is that like? Stay in the experience as long as you want to. Imagine yourself as another character in the story. What is that like?

Now open your journal and write about your experience. What was it like for you? What did you learn about the character of God? You can come back to this passage and do this several times in the weeks ahead if you want to. Ask God to continue to show Himself to you. Begin to pray Ephesians 1: 17, "that the God of our Lord Jesus Christ, the Father of glory may give you a spirit of wisdom and of revelation in the knowledge of Him." Ask Him to open your eyes to understand who He really is. He will do it!

Assignment Two: Expressing Gratitude

A heart connection with God is the foundation of an intimate relationship with other people. As we know and connect with God, we have more ability to connect with people. We need each other to celebrate our successes and to encourage us to get back on the path when we fall. In Ecclesiastes 4:9, the Bible says that "two are better than one...because if they fall, one will lift up his fellow." And again in Hebrews 10:24-25 God says, "and let us consider how to stir up one another to love and good works, ... encouraging one another..." Recovery is a journey that we make with friends.

Just as meditation changes the chemical composition of the brain, researchers are finding that doing selfless acts of service changes the brain to combat depression, despondency and addiction. Alcoholics Anonymous encourages giving back to those who are not as far along in recovery. What the research is finding is that it is not just a nice thing to do; it actually changes the chemical composition of the brain, making it more stable and functional.

Think for a moment about the people who have helped you in your journey. There are people who have supported you in your recovery. There are probably people who have impacted you in younger years in a significant way; think about family members, teachers, and friends. Now think for a moment about what they did that made a difference for you. Was it their attitude or something they physically did such as giving you a hug when you needed one or staying up late talking to you because you were upset? What are the character qualities of the people who have impacted you the most? Are there any similarities?

Exercises:

1. List the character qualities of the people who have helped you along the way.

____

____

____

2. Pick the three people who have had the most influence on you. List their names and what they did.

____

____

____

____

____

____

3. Write each of them a thank you note expressing your gratitude for what they mean to you and for what they did to help you. Feel free to write as many people on your list as you want to write but be sure to write at least three.

4. Develop a habit of thanking people and encouraging them in their journey. Thank one person each day for a week. Try to do it every day for a month. Ask God to help you to develop this habit. Learn to look for what is good in people and encourage them. It is amazing how much better you will feel about yourself when you do this. There is a principle in the Bible that you reap what you sow. If you sow thanksgiving and encouragement, you will reap thanks and encouragement back from others.

Assignment Three: Making A Plan For Recovery

In assignment three you will be working on the last part of Principle Six, addressing our weaknesses. In recovery, everyone needs a relapse prevention plan. In Principle Five, you had a specific plan for how to make amends for your past behavior. Now, in Principle Six, you want to make a specific plan for how deal with sexual temptation and maintain healthy behaviors. Change doesn't just happen. In the aftermath of Hurricane Katrina in New Orleans, the mayor kept saying that he *hoped* the Federal government would get there to help and he *hoped* that the state government would help. Anderson Cooper remarked, "Hope is not a plan."

There are four general areas that need to be addressed when making a plan for recovery. These areas are: emotional, physical, spiritual and relational. It is important to think about each area and note the places where you need to make some changes. Some suggestions for each area are listed below. You will probably come up with items of your own that need to be added to the list. Think about it and then talk it over with your accountability partners. Pray and ask God to help you.

Physical

Balanced diet
Adequate sleep
Exercise
Personal hygiene (bathing, brushing teeth)
Being responsible with possessions (taking care of your room or living space)
Develop a hobby that you've always wanted to do
Develop healthy work habits
Seek help in learning how to manage money
Avoid substitutes for sexual acting out (excessive smoking and drinking)

Emotional

Develop an awareness of feelings, attitudes, and mood changes
Seek counseling if necessary
Understand emotional triggers. Know what "sets you off"
Know your limitations.
Develop a realistic understanding and acceptance of what you can and can't accomplish
Ask for what you need emotionally in a healthy manner
Spend time healing wounds described in the cycle of addiction (Principle One)
Develop a habit of being thankful

Relational

Make phone calls to people in your group
Stay connected with people who'll support you in your goals
Be committed to helping others in their battle with sexual temptation
Share your story with safe people
Service to others; encouraging and affirming others

Spiritual

Prayer
Devotional time
Bible study
Develop a habit of being thankful
Reading spiritual materials
Spending time meditating on scriptures
Engaging in spiritual discussions with people in recovery
Develop a personal relationship with God

Using the suggestions above, make a list of things you want to do to grow in each of these areas. You might want to produce a daily checklist to see how you're doing. Chart your progress for the next four weeks and see how much change you begin to notice. Let this serve as a "before and after" picture for your first month of practice. Take note of the areas you did well in and the areas where you need more practice. Don't give up. This is only the beginning. Share the results with your mentor and accountability group.

Exercise:

Now make a list of the areas that you need to change. Come up with a plan for making that change. What will you do differently? Be specific. Remember, goals need to be specific and measurable. How will you know if you are changing? An example of a specific, measurable goal is: I will read one Bible verse a day and meditate on it for 15 minutes. A goal that is not specific and measurable is: I will read my Bible more.

____

____

Make a long term plan for the things that you want to change. Then choose one thing out of each area that you want to begin with. Trying to make too many changes at once can be overwhelming and self defeating. Make a daily checklist for yourself so that you can track and monitor your progress. Keep a record of each week for a month. At the end of the month, choose something to add to your checklist. Keep doing the behaviors that you have already been doing for the month. Soon you will have added all the things that you want to change. Remember, when you are making changes, don't forget to note the areas where you are making progress and the areas where you are doing well. Every move towards staying sober is worthy of celebration!

Take a moment to identify what you are feeling. Use the Feeling Words on page 109 if needed.

Principle Seven

As we live in sexual integrity, we carry the message of Christ's healing to those who still struggle, and we pursue a vision of God's purpose for our lives.

Finding a Purpose: I Have a Vision

*Jamie told her youth pastor that she had been asked to go clubbing with some of her friends from school. They were going to hook up with some guys they had met earlier in the week. "You know", she said, "I chose not to go because I really want to live a sober life and honor God. I thought I was going to look like a complete **** . But you know what happened? When I said no, one of the other girls asked me if I could talk to her later. She wanted me to help her change the way she was living. It made me feel really good to know that I could help someone else."*

One of the promises of A.A. is, "No matter how far down the scale we have gone, we will see how our experience can benefit others." You might think that you have done so many things that you are ashamed of that God could never use you. But that is not true. You are the very one that other strugglers will believe. As you walk this journey of recovery, you give hope to other women and girls that they can change too. They know it is possible when they see you. When you think about it, who do you want to talk to about your problems, someone who also struggles or someone who seems to have it all together? It is harder for them to believe someone who has never experienced the pain of sexual sin.

Assignment One: Sharing Your Journey

In order to do this assignment, you need to have at least six weeks of sobriety. If you do not have that, in other words, you have acted out in the last six weeks, then go back and work through Principle One and Four again. One of the mistakes that we make in recovery is encouraging people to give their testimony who are not far enough along in their sobriety. There is no shame in working through the principles again. Remember, the goal is sobriety. Keep going until you get there! If you are struggling with sexual sobriety, then here are some questions to ask yourself before you go through Principle One again. Discuss your answers with your accountability group. Ask them for any insight they might have into your situation.

1. Are you willing? Do you want to get well? Are you resisting the hard work that is necessary to maintain your sobriety? Are you giving up when it gets hard?

2. Have you surrendered your life and sexuality to Christ? Are there parts that you are holding onto? If you are not fully surrendered to Christ, talk to your mentor or pastor about what might be holding you back. I usually find that people who are not fully surrendered do not trust that God is good and that He can satisfy every longing of their heart.

3. Have you confessed all your sins? Are there things that are just too shameful or painful to expose? Are you hiding? Are you pretending?

4. Are you developing relationships with others who can help you maintain your sexual integrity? Are you isolated and keeping your distance from others? Are you telling the truth to your accountability group? Is your life an open book with them? Are you open to feedback from others?

For those of you who have at least six weeks of sexual sobriety, this assignment prepares you to carry the message to those who still struggle. Think for a moment about how you might carry the message. You can speak at a meeting. You might talk to a group at church or school. Others of you can talk to a friend or bring another person struggling with an addiction to a group meeting. Everyone has unique abilities and a unique testimony. Think about the gifts that God has given you and use them in telling your story. Are you better at speaking or writing? Do you have artistic or musical talent? Do you like to serve? Can you think of places where you can serve and tell your story as you work?

There is no right way to tell your story. But here are some tips to help you tell it in a way that will enable others to get the most out of it. You want to make it as concise as possible- tell the main points without going into a lot of detail. Don't be graphic in your explanations. Keep it to about 10 minutes. People have a hard time listening to someone for longer than that. You will want to cover three main areas: your acting out; how you stopped; and how your life is now.

In the first part, talk about your behavior that was out of control but be general. You may want to group behaviors under general categories such as pornography or hooking up in internet chat rooms. You may want to include as background any wounds that you had that set you up to act out. But one word of caution; you do not want to send a message that you are blaming your behavior on what happened to you. You want to take responsibility for your actions and encourage your listeners to do so as well. Talk about your efforts to stop the behavior and the consequences to you and others for not stopping.

Then tell what happened when you finally stopped and surrendered the addiction. What were your feelings? How did you finally stop the cycle of addiction? What was different this time? Talk about the journey that you have taken as you work on your sobriety each day. What are the most important parts of that journey? Have you failed along the way? You might want to share that because it is an important part of the journey.

Finally, tell what your life is like now. What is different? How have you seen God change you? How have your feelings changed about yourself and others? About God? Talk about the hope that you have for the future. Share your gratitude for what God and other people have done for you.

Now prayerfully consider who you can share your story with. Try to come up with 2 people or groups that you can tell your story to. Talk to your accountability group and make sure that the people and situations that you have in mind are safe. You want to practice having healthy boundaries. You do not need to tell your story to everyone. Wisdom is knowing when to talk and when to be quiet. God will help you if you ask Him. James 1:5 says, "If any of you lacks wisdom, let him ask God, who gives generously to all without reproach, and it will be given him."

Now it is time to step out and carry the message to others. Practice telling your story with your accountability group. Get feedback. Begin to pray and ask God to open the door for you to share with the 2 people or groups that you listed. This is not about performance; it is about sharing from your heart. Don't get all caught up in "getting it right". Some of the best testimonies I have ever heard were short and fumbling but heart-felt. People will know the difference between someone with a slick presentation and someone who is sincere. Just relax, be real, and talk from your heart.

Assignment Two: Creating A Vision

In preparing to tell your story, you have been focusing on the past. This is a necessary part of recovery. You have been going to meetings and talking about recovery for awhile now. It probably feels like that is all you do at times! But your life will not always be about these things. There is more to life than recovery. You are in the stage of life developmentally where your task is to form an identity, to know who you are. Yes, you are a person who has struggled with sexual integrity, but that is just a part of who you are; you are so much more than that. This is an exciting time for you as you begin to discover and become the person that you are created to be, with all your unique gifts, abilities and passions.

Part of that discovery is having a vision for your future. It is important to think about what you want your life to be like because the decisions you make today will in large part determine that future. So it is important to have an idea of who you want to be and what you want to be doing. You don't have to know exactly what you will be doing, but you can know what kind of person you want to be. And this is not a one time event. Your vision is fluid, it changes as you develop and mature. And God gives us different seasons of our lives, so the vision for one season might be different than the one for another season. The important thing is to begin to think about it. A vision is the picture of where you want to be 5, 10, 15 years from now. If you have that picture, then it will be easier to make decisions that will help you attain that vision. By keeping the picture before you, you will be encouraged and inspired to keep going.

For years sports psychologists have been helping athletes to visualize the races that they are going to run in order to help them focus and do their best. It helps them to keep the goal in mind and to run toward that goal. Interestingly, God tells us the same thing in Hebrews 12 (The Message), "…start running-and never quit ...keep your eyes on Jesus, who both began and finished this race we're in." and in Proverbs He says, "As a man thinks in his heart, so is he." What we think about and focus on determines in large part the person that we become. If you focus on Jesus, you will become more like Him. As people we are all created to worship. We will either worship God or something else. There are many ways that we choose to worship something else. Addiction is one of those ways. But at heart, we are all looking for what God has wired us to only get from Him. As Augustine says, Our hearts are satisfied when they find their rest in Him. The good news is that it is not all up to us. According to Philippians 1:6, *God* will complete what He started in you. Pray and ask God to help you with your vision. What is His vision for this season of your life? If you focus on Jesus and keep that vision before you, then God will empower you to move towards it. And in the process, you will be changed.

Exercises:

1. Begin to think about your vision. What kind of person do you want to be? In other words, what are the character traits of the person that you want to be?

____

____

____

____

____

____

2. What are the character traits that other people notice about you now?

____

____

____

____

____

____

3. What gifts and abilities do you have? What things have other people commented on?

____

____

____

____

____

____

4. What do you see yourself doing? What are you passionate about? What do you dream about doing or being? Many times, around the age of 11, girls quit dreaming. They begin to believe that they do not have anything to contribute. This is a part of the cultural wounds that we talked about earlier. If you are having trouble with this assignment, try to remember what you wanted to be and what your dreams were when you were a little girl. Don't be embarrassed, brainstorm. God has put dreams in all of us. You just need to unlock those dreams.

____

____

____

____

____

____

5. God does not waste anything. Have you thought about that? The time that you spent in sexual sin is not wasted. Your recovery is not wasted. God uses everything to make us the people He wants us to be. What do you think you have learned from your sexual sin and recovery that might be a part of your vision?

____

____

____

____

____

____

In ancient times, sailors would navigate by the stars. As long as they could see the stars, they could get to their destination. The vision you develop is like the stars to those ancient mariners. If you keep it before you, you can get to your destination. The Lord bless you as you pray and seek His vision for your life.

Assignment Three: Tying It All Together

Congratulations! You are almost finished. Take a moment and look back over the last weeks and months as you have worked through the assignments in this book. Be sure to give yourself credit for all the hard work you have done. It has not been easy. I'm sure that there have been painful moments for you. But you have persevered.

Exercise:

Journal about these questions. How does it feel to be near the end? What feelings are coming up for you now? What changes do you see in yourself? How have you grown? Are there areas where you still need to improve?

Remember the Carnes cycle of addiction? We have spent time looking at the components of the cycle in detail. It begins with the wounded self. These wounds come from family or culture. These wounds lead to shame. In order to deal with the shame, an addict begins to fantasize, which then leads to rituals and acting out. After acting out, despair sets in which leads to a lowered mood. So how do you raise your mood? You begin fantasizing again and the cycle repeats itself.

That is the cycle of addiction. But now we want to look at the Laaser cycle of recovery. Whereas the cycle of addiction leads to despair, the cycle of recovery leads to joy. Notice the components of the recovery cycle printed on next page.

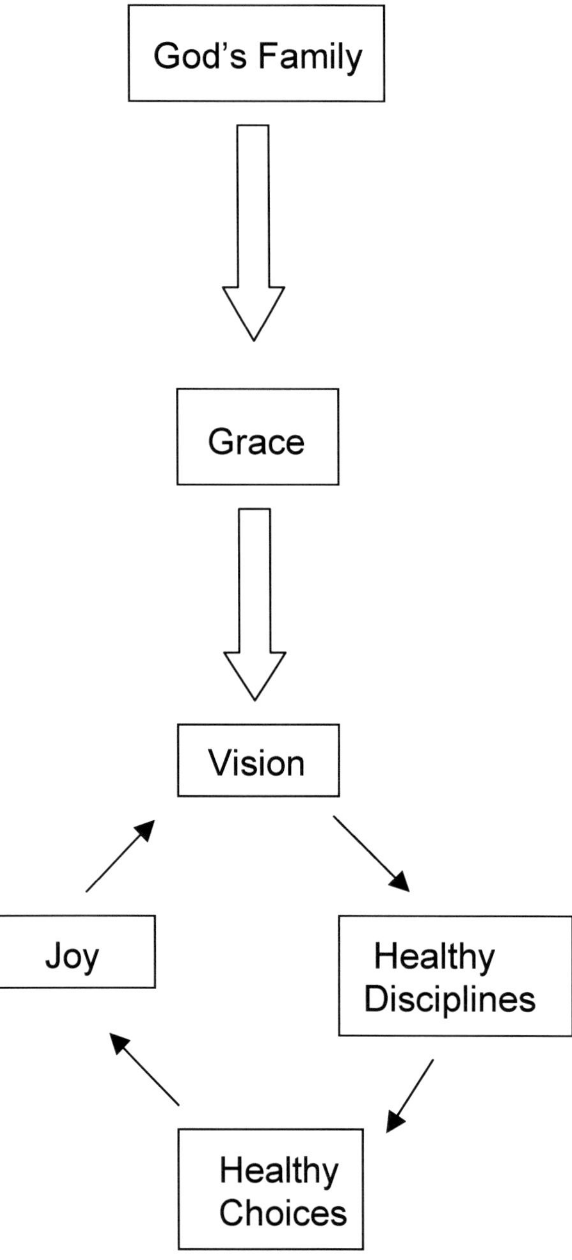

Whereas the addiction cycle begins with wounds from family and culture, the recovery cycle begins with God and His family. We have talked about the longing to be connected with people in authentic relationship. Hopefully, you have begun to experience the healing that comes from being a part of a group of people where you can be real and vulnerable and they still love and support you. Maybe you have found this in your family. But for many, the church becomes the healing family that they never had. Maybe it is your accountability group which is a part of your community of faith. Intimacy with God and other people is the foundation for recovery and healing.

When you begin to understand how much God loves and delights in you and then have that fleshed out in a community of people who love and accept you, then God's grace takes on new meaning. It truly becomes good news. You see more clearly God's heart for you and for other people who struggle. As you get your needs met by God and your community of safe people, you will find that the desire to fantasize becomes less and is gradually replaced by a stronger sense of vision.

The vision then is the roadmap for the healthy disciplines and healthy choices that you make. These can be as varied as exercise, changing the way you eat, doing homework, playing music, calling a friend or practicing spiritual disciplines. In Principle Six, you practiced the spiritual discipline of meditation. There are other disciplines that you can begin to practice that will help you in this journey. Some suggestions are prayer, reading your Bible, silence, service and giving. Do some reading on spiritual disciplines and begin to practice one that appeals to you. Remember, discipline just sets you up for success. God is the one who changes you, not your own self effort. But healthy disciplines lead to healthy choices instead of sexual acting out. And healthy choices produce joy which leads to a clearer vision of what you were created to be and a clearer picture of your place in this adventure of life.

Exercise:

Think through a time when you acted out sexually. Now mentally work through the steps of the recovery cycle using that situation. What are the different steps that you could have taken at each step of the cycle? Imagine doing those steps and having a different outcome. Take time to visualize making those different choices. Journal your feelings as you think about the future.

Well done! You are well on your way to a life of living in freedom everyday. May the Lord give you great joy as you experience more and more the depth of His love for you. You are a dearly loved daughter. In Romans 15:13, Paul prays "May the God of hope fill you with all joy and peace in believing, so that by the power of the Holy Spirit you may abound in hope." This is my prayer for you.

Take a moment to identify what you are feeling. Use the Feeling Words on page 109 if needed.

Appendix A

FEELING WORDS FOR YOUR JOURNEY

LOVE, CONCERN

admired	adorable	accepted	affectionate	agreeable	appreciated
benevolent	benign	brotherly	caring	charitable	comforting
compassionate	content	congenial	conscientious	considerate	cordial
courteous	dedicated	devoted	empathetic	fair	faithful
forgiving	friendly	generous	genuine	giving	good
helpful	honest	honorable	hospitable	humane	interested
just	kind	kindly	lenient	lovable	loving
mellow	mild	confident	neighborly	nice	obliging
open	optimistic	patient	peaceful	pleasant	polite
reasonable	receptive	reliable	respectful	relaxed	responsible
sensitive	sympathetic	sweet	tender	thoughtful	tolerant
truthful	trustworthy	understanding	unselfish	warm	whole
wonderful					

JOY, GLAD

alive	blissful	brilliant	calm	cheerful	comical
contented	delighted	ecstatic	elated	elevated	enchanted
enthusiastic	exalted	excellent	excited	fantastic	fit
gay	glad	glorious	good	grand	gratified
great	happy	humorous	inspired	jovial	joyful
jubilant	magnificent	majestic	marvelous	pleased	pleasant
proud	satisfied	splendid	superb	terrific	thrilled
tremendous	triumphant	vivacious	wonderful	vital	

COMPETENT

able	adequate	assured	authoritative	bold	brave
capable	confident	courageous	determined	durable	dynamic
effective	energetic	fearless	firm	forceful	gallant
hardy	healthy	heroic	important	influential	intense
manly	mighty	powerful	robust	secure	sharp
skillful	spirited	stable	stouthearted	strong	sure
tough	virile				

DEPRESSION, SADNESS

abandoned	agitated	alien	alienated	alone	awful
battered	blue	burned	cheapened	crushed	debased
defeated	despair	estranged	excluded	exhausted	forlorn
forsaken	fragile	gloomy	glum	grim	guilt
hopeless	horrible	humiliated	hurt	jilted	kaput
lonely	lousy	low	miserable	mistreated	moody
mournful	ostracized	pathetic	pitiful	rebuke	regretful
rejected	reprimanded	rotten	ruined	run down	stranded
tearful	terrible	unhappy	unloved	whipped	worthless
wrecked	wounded	victimized			

ANXIETY, FEAR

afraid	agitated	alarmed	anxious	apprehensive	bashful
concerned	desperate	dreadful	embarrassed	fearful	fidgety
frantic	frightened	hesitant	horrified	insecure	intimidated
jealous	jittery	jumpy	nervous	on edge	overwhelmed
panicky	perturbed	restless	scared	shaky	shy
strained	tense	terrified	threatened	timid	uncomfortable
uneasy	worrying				

DISTRESS

afflicted	alone	anguish	awkward	baffled	bewildered
clumsy	confused	constrained	crushed	defeated	disgusted
disliked	displeased	dissatisfied	distrustful	disturbed	doubtful
foolish	fragile	futile	grief	helpless	hindered
hopeless	impaired	impatient	imprisoned	lost	nauseated
offended	pained	perplexed	puzzled	rejected	ridiculous
sickened	skeptical	speechless	strained	suspicious	unsatisfied
unsure	worried				

INADEQUATE

anemic	broken	cowardly	crippled	defective	deficient
demoralized	disabled	exhausted	exposed	fragile	frail
helpless	inadequate	incapable	incompetent	ineffective	inept
inferior	insecure	meek	powerless	puny	shaken
sickly	small	trivial	unable	uncertain	unfit
unimportant	unqualified	unsound	useless	vulnerable	weak

GUILT & SHAME

ashamed	abused	bad	degraded	detested	disgraced
failure	humiliated	ignored	regretful	rejected	unimportant
ugly	unloved	stupid	tormented	worthless	

ANGER

agitated	aggravated	aggressive	angry	annoyed	arrogant
belligerent	biting	blunt	bullying	callous	combative
cool	cranky	critical	cross	cruel	disagreeable
disgusted	displeased	envious	fierce	furious	hard
harsh	hostile	impatient	inconsiderate	indifferent	irritated
insensitive	intolerant	mad	mean	nasty	obstinate
provoked	savage	severe	spiteful	upset	uptight
unsound	useless	vengeful	vicious	vindictive	violent
vulnerable	wrath				

Appendix B

Identity

Healing for the Nations

I AM ACCEPTED BY GOD

It is written… I am accepted by God, secure eternally!

MY HEAVENLY FATHER SAYS…

Acts 13:38 *I have forgiveness of sins through Christ.*

Romans 5:1 *I have been justified by faith and have peace with God through Jesus Christ.*

Romans 5:10 *I have been saved by Jesus' life.*

ROMANS 6:2 *I have died to sin, therefore I no longer want to live in sin.*

ROMANS 6:3 *I have been baptized into Christ's death.*

Hebrews 13:5 *God will never desert me nor forsake me.*

1 PETER 1:4 *I have obtained an inheritance which is imperishable and undefiled and will not fade away, reserved in heaven for me.*

1 PETER 1:18-19 *I was not redeemed with perishable things like silver or gold, but with precious blood, as of a lamb unblemished and spotless—the blood of Christ.*

ROMANS 6:6 *I have been crucified with Christ and the body of sin has been destroyed so I do not serve sin.*

ROMANS 8:1 *I am no longer condemned.*

1 CORINTHIANS 1:9 *I am called into fellowship with Jesus Christ my Lord.*
JOHN 3:16 I have everlasting life.

II CORINTHIANS 1:4 *I am comforted by God in all my troubles.*

II CORINTHIANS 1:22 *I have been given the Holy Spirit as a pledge (deposit), guaranteeing my future in Him.*

LAMENTATIONS 3:22-23 *I have received God's mercy, His compassion, and His faithfulness.*

II CORINTHIANS 5:1 *I have a house not made by hands, eternal in heaven.*

II CORINTHIANS 5:18 *I have the ministry of reconciliation.*

EPHESIANS 1:5 *Because of God's will and good pleasure, I am an adopted child of God through Jesus Christ.*

EPHESIANS 1:6 *I am accepted in the Beloved.*

EPHESIANS 1:11 *I have been chosen by God.*

EPHESIANS 1:7 *Because of God's grace, I have redemption and forgiveness of my sins.*

EPHESIANS 2:4 *God loves me.*

EPHESIANS 2:5 *I have been made alive together with Christ.*

EPHESIANS 2:6 *I have been raised up with Him and seated with Him in the heavenly places with Christ Jesus.*

EPHESIANS 2:8 *I have been saved by grace, through faith, not by any works I have done.*

EPHESIANS 2:13 *I have been brought near to God by the blood of Jesus.*

EPHESIANS 2:14 *Christ is my peace; He has destroyed the barrier between God and me.*

EPHESIANS 2:18 *Through Christ we have our access to the Father by one spirit.*

EPHESIANS 2:19 *I am no longer a stranger and an alien, but I am a fellow-citizen with the saints and a member of God's household.*

EPHESIANS 3:12 *By faith in Jesus Christ, I have freedom and confident access to God.*

EPHESIANS 4:32 *I have been forgiven by God for Christ's sake.*

PHILIPPIANS 1:6 *I am confident that He Who began a good work in me will perfect it until the day of Christ Jesus.*

PHILIPPIANS 1:21 *For to me, to live is Christ.*

PHILIPPIANS 2:13 *God is at work within me both to will and to work for His good pleasure.*

PHILIPPIANS 4:7 *The peace of God guards my heart and mind in Christ Jesus.*

COLOSSIANS 1:14 *Because of Jesus Christ, I have redemption and forgiveness of sins.*

COLOSSIANS 2:13 *Jesus Christ has made me alive.*

COLOSSIANS 2:14 *All my sin debt was paid in full at the cross.*

COLOSSIANS 3:3 *I have died to sin and my life is hidden with Christ in God.*

GALATIANS 2:20 *Christ lives in me and now I live by faith in the Son of God.*

COLOSSIANS 3:10 *I have put on the new self, which is being renewed in knowledge in the image of our Creator God.*

I THESSALONIANS 2:12 *I am called into God's kingdom and Glory, and I am to live in a manner worthy of that calling.*

I THESSALONIANS 4:17 *I will live forever with the Lord.*

I THESSALONIANS 5:9 *I have salvation by the Lord Jesus Christ.*

I THESSALONIANS 5:10 *Whether I live or die, I will live with Jesus.*

I THESSALONIANS 5:23-24 *Jesus has called me and He is faithful.*

II THESSALONIANS 2:13 *I am beloved by the Lord. God has chosen me from the beginning for salvation through sanctification by the Spirit and belief in the truth.*

II TIMOTHY 1:9 *The Lord has saved me and called me to live a holy life – not according to my works, but according to His own purpose and grace which was given to me in Christ Jesus for all eternity (before the beginning of time.)*

II TIMOTHY 1:12 *I am convinced that He is able to guard what I have entrusted to Him until that day (of death.)*

II TIMOTHY 4:8 *The Lord has laid up for me the crown of righteousness.*

TITUS 2:14 *Jesus has redeemed me from every lawless deed and is purifying me for His own possession.*

TITUS 3:7 *I have been justified by God's grace and made an heir according to the hope of eternal life.*

I JOHN 3:22 *Because I keep God's commandments and do the things that are pleasing in His sight whatever I ask I receive from Him.*

I PETER 2:10 *I am part of the family of God and I have received mercy.*

I PETER 2:9 *Because of Jesus Christ's atoning death on the cross, I am chosen, a royal priest, part of a holy nation, a person belonging to God. Therefore I praise Him Who called me out of sin and darkness and into His wonderful light.*

Definitions

Communication is essential to intimate relationships. It's important to not shame yourself or another group member over incorrect usage of words. Remember, we have all been subjected to misinformation from misguided peers and culture about sexuality. Group members might have an abundance of incorrect information or very little information. Both ignorance and saturation can lead to the same result - unhealthy sexuality. Group discussion, feedback, and presentations are important in helping us communicate and understand ourselves and each other. Therefore, we need to speak the same language. Developing a correct and godly use of terms can assist in the healing process from sexual addiction. Standard terminology is a tool for clear communication, and agreement about definitions allows each L.I.F.E. Group member to communicate easily with others in his own group and in the ministry network across the country. Each group member should study the following definitions to eliminate as much confusion as possible in regard to terminology. (These definitions may also provide a productive discussion topic for a L.I.F.E. Group meeting.) The definitions are based on my understanding gleaned from talking to hundreds of recovering people from a variety of geographic locations. Every group, though, may have local or personal understandings that are important in their setting. What's crucial is that the group discusses variations in meanings so that everyone can be clear about them.

Abstinence

This is the state of being non-sexual with self or others. Sometimes this may include a planned time-out from any romantic relationship

Accountability Partner

This is any person who agrees to be in your network of people holding you accountable. It will probably be someone other than your parents. The word "partner" implies more mutuality in the relationship than you would have with an authority figure.

Acting Out/Acting In

"Acting out" refers to engaging in sinful or dysfunctional behaviors, in this case, sexual behaviors. "Acting in" refers to rigidly controlling sexual behaviors in an unhealthy way. It often means that sex (or some other behavior) is being strictly avoided, but the person isn't growing emotionally and spiritually. "Acting out" and "acting in" are opposite ends of the same continuum. They can both be attempts to control painful memories, emotions, temptations, or experiences.

Addiction

Historically, the word "addiction" has been controversial in the Christian community. Some fear the concept of addiction removes personal responsibility for sinful behavior. Some believe those who call themselves addicts blame their personal decisions on an "addiction." The addict who is humble, desires to change, and accepts personal responsibility for his actions will not blame the disease of addiction for his choices. The concept of addiction is a way to understand why certain behaviors take place and why they are more difficult to manage.

The medical and psychological community has several universal criteria for determining if a substance or a behavior is an addiction:

1. **Use of the substance or behavior has become "unmanageable."** This means that the addict has tried repeatedly to stop but can't. The word "powerless" has been used to describe this pattern. Sometimes addicts feel "out of control." The addict isn't able to stop the destructive behavior, even in the face of deadly consequences.

2. **The addiction gets worse over time.** This means that more and more of the substance or behavior will be needed to achieve the same effect. An alcoholic knows that as he continues to drink he will need more and more alcohol to get "high" or drunk. Sex addicts know that they need more and more sexual activity to achieve the same "high" of the acting out experience. The increase of behavior may involve doing more and more of the same behavior. It could also involve a progression to new kinds of acting out experiences. For example, one might go from masturbating with pictures over the Internet to a sexual relationship with another person. In rare cases, it can progress to dangerous and illegal activity. Sexual addicts may be able to stop behaviors for periods of times, but until they find healing, it will always return to them. Over time, a repeated pattern of failure will be evident.

3. **Tolerance is one reason for the factor of progression.** Medical science is discovering new things about the human brain that broaden our understanding of addiction. The chemistry of the brain will adjust to whatever an addict puts into it. Over time, the brain demands more to achieve to same effect. For alcoholics, the brain adjusts to alcohol and requires more. Thinking about sex and engaging in sexual behavior requires that the brain produce the brain chemistry needed to achieve sexual response. New research is finding that sexual chemistry of the brain can also become tolerant, which means more and more thought or activity is necessary to have the same brain chemistry effects - the feelings of arousal, excitement, and pleasure. In many ways, sex addicts are drug addicts, because they become high on the drug produced in their own brain.

4. **Because of the brain chemistry involved, addicts use the thoughts and behaviors that produce the neurochemical highs to either raise or lower their mood.** We sometimes say that addicts "medicate" their feelings. If an addict is depressed, lonely, or bored, he can think exciting sexual thoughts, either of real experiences or fantasies, and his brain will produce the chemicals to alter the mood. The associated

brain chemicals create a feeling of well-being and contentment that lowers his mood. Most addicts can use sexual thoughts or activities to raise and lower their mood.

5. **Finally, addicts act out despite negative consequences.** Addicts enter a state called "denial" and don't pay attention to negative consequences. They will often "minimize" or "rationalize" their acting out, despite the consequences. Until an addict decides to surrender control of his fears that prevent him from getting help, he'll continue to act out. Addicts may also continue to act out because it's usually a slow and insidious form of death. They know at an intellectual level that they are destroying themselves and others, but the addiction keeps them from caring.

Affairs

Relationships of a sexual or emotional nature that involve a partner to whom you're not married.

Anonymous Sex

Having a sexual relationship with someone whose name isn't known and with whom no relationship exists.

Bottom Line

A "bottom line" is a boundary that refers to which behaviors are acceptable and which ones aren't. A man who struggles with Internet pornography might have a bottom line behavior of not surfing the web without the presence of an accountability partner or no compulsive masturbation.

Boundaries

In simple terms, boundaries are limits that are set for safety. They define behavior that should and should not take place. They are necessary to avoid harm to yourself in your journey of transformation. Unhealthy boundaries may be either "too loose" or "too rigid". Healthy boundaries keep bad things out while allowing good things in. (Stating your boundaries is a way of asking for safety.)

Codependency

This term was first used to describe those in close relationships with alcoholics. A codependent might be anyone who tolerates problematic or addictive behavior. It has also been described as "relationship addiction." The more people crave the approval and presence of an addict, the more likely they are to ignore their own needs and sacrifice themselves. They may claim to be sacrificing in love, but in reality, they are sacrificing out of their own fears and insecurities. Codependents often "enable" an addict by making excuses for him or her and generally looking the other way. A codependent may try to save an addict from consequences. It has also been described as "approval addiction."

Compartmentalizing

James 4:8 refers to a man who is "double-minded." This term means various parts of ourselves can be at war with one another. We "dissociate" from trying to think about behavior. An addict may compartmentalize behavior and deny that it even exists in reality.

Cross Talk

This is simply talking back and forth in meetings. Groups struggle with this if one member dominates the group by talking too long, giving too much advice, or being angry, judgmental, or simply rude. L.I.F.E. Group members need to be good listeners and not amateur counselors. Healthy cross talk is a part of L.I.F.E. Groups that provides essential support and relationship building.

Cruising

This term refers to any ritual behavior (described in Principle 1 Assignment 2) which is designed to find a partner or to act out sexually. Cruising rituals can involve dress, appearance, facial expressions, flirting, "hanging out" in certain places, or any variety of behaviors to find or attract a partner.

Cycle

A cycle is a predictable pattern where one thought or behavior leads to others that eventually lead back to the original thought or behavior. The cycle of addiction is explained in Principle 1 Assignment 2.

Denial

Denial is avoiding reality. Fear of consequences, reactions of others, or painful emotions are the usual causes for avoiding the truth. Denial can involve direct lies or the avoidance of reality.

Entitlement

All addicts have a need to "excuse" their behaviors. They need a reason to "act out." There is a "balance sheet" in their heads that says when they have done enough "good behaviors" they are entitled to some "bad behaviors." Some addicts feel so unjustly treated in life, like martyrs, that they believe it's only fair for them to get something for themselves. Anger and narcissism fuel the feeling of entitlement.

Family of Origin

Your family of origin generally refers to your immediate biological family: your parents and brothers and sisters. It can also mean any people who have lived with you under the same roof. Examples may include stepparents, aunts, uncles, cousins, grandparents. The term can also include others who lived with you, even if they aren't biologically related.

Fantasy

Fantasy is thinking about anything in an imaginary way. Sexual fantasy is entertaining thoughts about imagined sex, either about past experiences or "hoped for" experiences in the future.

Grooming

Grooming behaviors are behaviors intended to gain someone's trust and, therefore, may seem innocent. Both sexual predators and sexual addicts may engage in grooming potential victims or sexual partners.

Hooking Up

Casual sexual encounter, without commitment or connection. There can be one encounter between two people or multiple encounters over weeks and mouths between the same two people. Hooking up includes anything kissing through intercourse.

Intimacy Disorder

Intimacy is the ability of two people to be real with each other. Intimacy disorder is based on fear and anxiety. There is a fear that someone will leave us and anxiety that we will be all alone. This is based on two core beliefs of a sex addict. The two beliefs are that "I am a bad and worthless person" and that "no one will like me as I am." These are foundational ideas for sex addicts and codependents.

Masturbation

The act of stimulating one's own genitals for sexual arousal and orgasm. This is usually done with the use of fantasy or sexually explicit material such as magazines, books, or computer images.

Medicating

Medicating refers to using a substance or behavior to alter a mood.

Mentor

A mentor is an older person who can provide guidance, insight, and support in your journey of recovery from sexual acting out.

Minimizing

Similar to denial, minimizing literally means attempting to make smaller what is really true. A typical addict will minimize how destructive his behaviors are to himself and others.

Narcissism

This is a classical term based on the Greek figure Narcissus, a man who loved his own reflection. Narcissists will congratulate themselves on their own accomplishments and are very self-centered. Narcissists often seem very self-confident, but in reality they are very insecure. They lack self-confidence and try to bolster themselves.

Neurochemical

All activities of the brain are facilitated by the interaction of chemicals in the brain. What is sometimes called the electrical activity of the brain is based on chemistry, or "neurochemistry." Scientists have identified hundreds of chemicals involved in the process of "communication" among brain cells. Some people are born with genetic predispositions to having problems with the proper balance of these chemicals. Addictive and dysfunctional behavior can also alter the normal state of brain chemistry. Psychiatry is the medical science that seeks to understand the right balance and prescribe medications to correct such disorders.

Objectification

This literally means to view someone as an object rather than a person. Sexually, objectification means to see someone as only a physical body and not as a person with a mind and soul. Objectifying is de-humanizing. When we objectify someone, it's easier to lust after that person as just a body to be desired.

Oral Sex

Sexual activity involving oral stimulation of ones partners sex organs.

Prostitution

Prostitution is sex that is paid for. It can be bought over the phone, Internet, in massage parlors, on the streets, or through escort services.

Rationalization

This is an excuse or justification. Rationalizations are used to explain why something was or was not done.

Relapse

A relapse is a series of slips that reflect the crossing of emotional, spiritual, and sexual boundaries. A relapse is an on-going violation of sobriety.

Rubber-Necking

Turning your head to take in a sexual stimulus (usually another person) for a long period of time.

Sexual Anorexia

It involves inhibited sexual desire and complete abstinence from sexual activity. A person can be sexually anorexic with one person (a spouse) but still act out addictively with others.

Shame

A core belief of a sex addict is that "I am a bad and worthless person." This is a shame-based conviction. Unhealthy shame occurs when a person's life experiences, especially trauma, lead him to believe he doesn't deserve God's love. Healthy shame is felt when we know we need God.

Slip

A slip is a one-time violation of sobriety in any form. "Slip" is an acronym for "**S**hort **L**apse **I**n **P**rogress." A violation of sobriety means a "short lapse" only if the person learns from it, repents, and grows in understanding as a result.

Sobriety

In Christian morality, a state of sobriety exists when a person isn't being sexual with self or others outside of marriage in addictive form. This can also involve fantasy.

Sponsor

A sponsor is your main accountability partner. The qualities of a sponsor will be described throughout this book. A sponsor may be like a mentor - someone who has more experience in the journey of transformation toward sexual purity.

Trauma Bonding

It's a pattern of unhealthy attachments and relationships. To be trauma bonded means that two people are attracted to each other because of conscious or unconscious characteristics which remind them of earlier people in their lives who wounded them. It's based on the hope that if you keep repeating old behaviors you'll eventually get it right.

Trigger

There are two kinds of triggers in our program. It's generally assumed that the word trigger refers to the stimulation of inappropriate sexual desire or action. Any stimulus that can be seen, heard, felt, smelled, tasted, remembered, or fantasized about that creates sexual desire or action (even if only in the brain) is a sexual trigger. Any stimulus that causes emotional and spiritual feelings of anxiety, fear, loneliness, boredom, depression, or anger is a general trigger. Often general triggers are referred to as "emotional triggers." General triggers become sexual triggers when sex is used to medicate the feeling created by a general trigger.

A Final Word On Words

Words and meaning change over time. It isn't productive to spend group time arguing over words and definitions. Words are simply a tool to help us communicate. If there is a disagreement about some term, come to a group consensus and move forward.

In addition to these terms that I have defined, your group may encounter many others that I have not included. Please contact L.I.F.E. Ministries with terms you would like to know about, have a good definition for, or simply think should be included in future editions of this L.I.F.E. Guide.

Resources

Professional Counseling

Faithful and True Marriages	Led by Richard Blankenship and Heath Wise, this ministry offers intensive workshops and retreats for men, women, spouses, and couples in recovery from sexual addiction. These retreats and workshops are offered in various locations around the United States. Faithful and True Marriages is a cooperative effort between Faithful and True – Atlanta and L.I.F.E. Ministries International. www.faithfulandtruemarriages.com
Faithful and True Ministry	Led by Dr. Mark Laaser, this Twin Cities area ministry offers local counseling, intensive workshops, and Faithful and True support groups for sexual addicts and co-addicts in various locations around the country. www.faithfulandtrueministries.com
Faithful and True – Atlanta	Led by Richard Blankenship, M.Ed., M.A. LPC, NCC, CCSAS this Atlanta, Georgia based ministry offers individual, couples, and group counseling for male sexual addicts, female sexual addicts, spouses of sexual addicts, and couples retreats. www.christiansexualintegrity.org
Healing for the Nations	Offers biblical resources and has monthly Retreats and Conferences. The Intensive Retreat in an innovative retreat designed to encourage "head to heart" breakthroughs of God's Truths and equip people with powerful, life long discipleship tools. Located in Marietta, GA 1-800-483-2841 www.healingforthenations.org

Hospitals

The Meadows **While not Christian-based, the Meadows** offers a program with experts in treating sexual addiction.
www.themeadows.org

Sierra Tuscon — Sierra Tucson offers a wide range of programs for behavioral and chemical addictions.
www.sierratucson.com

Pine Grove — Treatment for sexual addiction is offered under the direction of Dr. Patrick Carnes.
www.pinegrovetreatment.com

Support Group Ministries

L.I.F.E. Ministries International
Bob & Johna Hale, Executive Director
Lake Mary, FL
Telephone: (407) 647-9560
www.freedomeveryday.org

Faithful and True Ministries
Dr. Mark Laaser, Director
Chanhassen, MN
Telephone: (952) 949-3478
www.faithfulandtrueministries.com

Celebrate Recovery
John Baker, Director
Mission Viejo, CA
Telephone (714) 581-9100

ABOUT THE AUTHOR

Heath Wise, M.A. is a professional counselor and a certified clinical sexual addiction specialist who works with the North Atlanta Center for Christian Counseling in Atlanta, Georgia. She works as a counselor with Faithful and True Atlanta , a ministry dedicated to providing resources for male sexual addicts, female sexual addicts, spouses (both male and female) of sexual addicts, and couples in recovery from sexual addiction. This is one of the few programs in the United States that also provides resources for the entire family, including teens (male and female) who struggle with sexual compulsivity.

Heath began her career as a lay counselor at her church working with survivors of childhood sexual abuse. She then earned a masters in professional counseling with a specialization in sex therapy from the Psychological Studies Institute in Atlanta, Georgia. She lectures on the subject of sexual addiction, sexual trauma and abuse as well as healthy sexuality at professional conferences, churches and schools.

Heath recently moved to Northern California to work with an organization that helps runaways and trafficked women and children. She continues to work with Faithful and True Atlanta as a therapist for the marriage retreats and addiction recovery workshops that they offer around the country.